ENGLISH HOUSES

SINCE FOR REFRESHMENT
ONE COMETH HENCE,
LET WIT CAST OFF THE
DEAR DULL YOKE OF SENSE

To my parents.

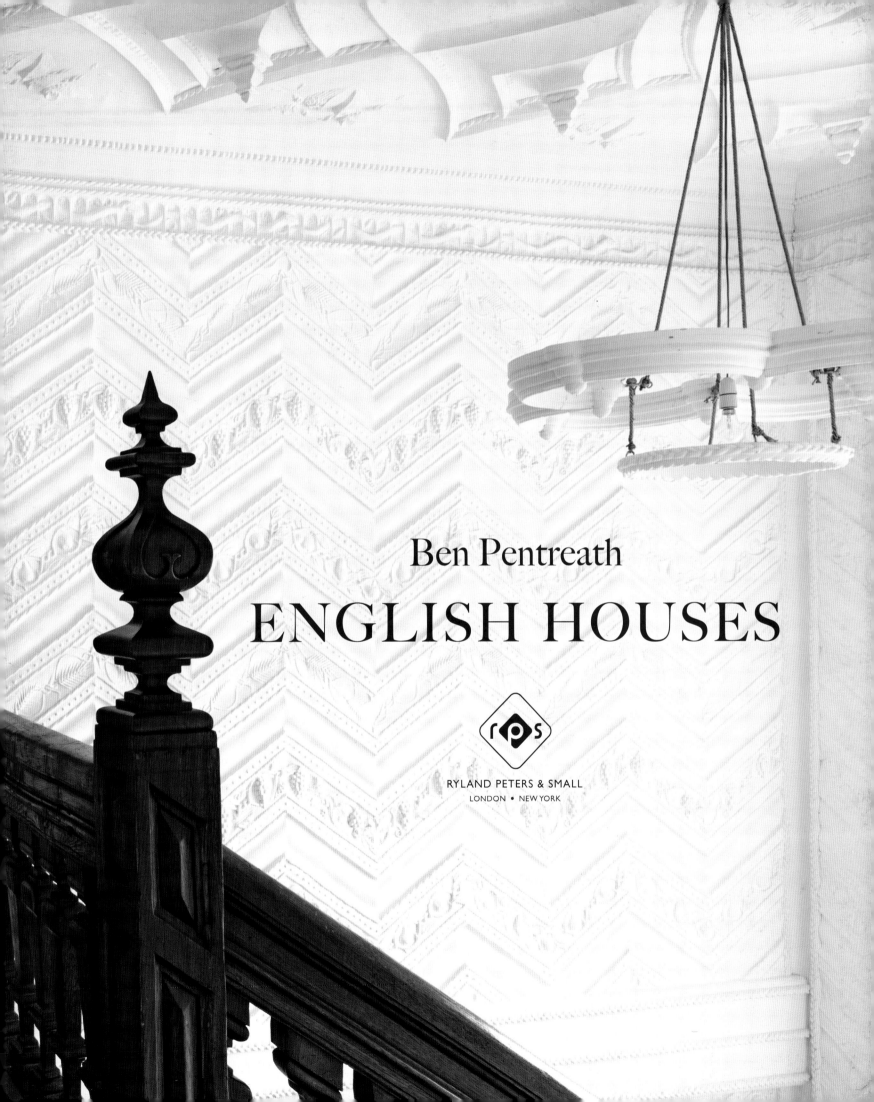

Ben Pentreath

ENGLISH HOUSES

RYLAND PETERS & SMALL
LONDON • NEW YORK

Contents

Introduction

THIS IS A BOOK ABOUT HOUSES, but more than that, it is a book about people and about time. I realize that when we think about the interiors of houses, we often start by concentrating on the architecture, or on the key pieces of furniture, or the rugs, pictures and lamps; colours, textures and incidental moments. But a perfectly decorated room without people to occupy it, love it, and live in it is meaningless; and a room without a sense of time and of evolution is as empty as a diary containing entirely blank pages.

Some of the interiors we will be looking at are very old and have the settled, drowsy air that only centuries of unhurried occupation can bequeath; others are brand new, still just fresh with the smell of paint, but even here we can detect a timelessness and a sense of personality that brings to life that elusive quality to which I refer.

Interiors, after all, can be momentary; they are far less durable than architecture and are subject to the whims of owners, of fashion, and of taste; their moment may be very brief— photographs of famous rooms can be far more enduring than the spaces themselves. Longevity is not necessarily the important ingredient. The final chapter of this book shows Trematon Castle, an ancient Cornish place, but the rooms that we will be looking at there were assembled less than five years ago by the brilliant, theatrical Julian and Isabel Bannerman, who understand better than anyone else the gentle art of making things look as if they have been there for ever.

I love, too, interiors that evolve. I am not a believer in rooms remaining fixed in aspic; neither am I a believer in the fact that it is possible to assemble a room in an instant and for it to feel anything other than like a hotel. In decorating my own houses—the Old Parsonage in Dorset and our flat in London—I realize how much things change over the years. The big structural alterations may last for a long time, but even then it is fun to shake things up, to move things around, and to make space for a new picture or pieces of furniture from the junk auction that you have no room for but couldn't live without. It's wonderful to pick up a paintbrush and start testing new colours on a familiar wall—as I write, Charlie and I are contemplating painting the walls of our Dorset kitchen in a bright buttercup gloss yellow. All this happens over time. It allows for mistakes and experiments, for shifts in mind or mood, and for change for the sake of, well… change. And all this is what makes life interesting!

Over the last four or five years I have become increasingly in demand as a professional decorator. I have to admit that my previous book, *English Decoration*, is partly to blame, for it has introduced me to one or two adventurous clients who understood—rather quickly, I suspect—that I had no formal training and yet with whom something I was writing about, or looking at, has sounded a chord.

But the world of professional 'Interior Design' is a challenging one. It expects results on a plate, which increasingly I realize is not possible to deliver—not if you believe in evolution. I think I noticed this early on, when I found that cushions or lampshades or, indeed, whole pieces of furniture carefully intended for one room felt far more at home elsewhere. This is the curious alchemy of putting together rooms. Who knows why cushions feel happier here rather than there. So I have learned to talk to my clients about taking things slowly; to bring in first the big pieces, which take care and thought, but then to let the little touches of life evolve and mature more gently.

It's not easy getting this right—and not least, I hasten to add, because there is no right and wrong in decoration. Architecture is simpler. I can tell you the correct thickness of a glazing bar, or proportions of a chimneypiece or shape of a moulding. But who am I to say 'this wall should be blue' or 'that chair should be orange' when the client may very well not

like blue or orange at all? Good decoration, after all, is a matter of opinion and not of fact; it's virtually impossible to write down rules, because any room we really love or admire, without doubt, flouts every rule in the book. So I suppose we are talking about combining feelings with experience in making judgements about what is most successful. A lot of the time these days I find my best role, as decorator, is as a collaborator, giving my clients the confidence and ability to explore their own ideas. One day, I may try to collate some of these thoughts into a book, but you will forgive me, I hope, if for now we just spend time in some sensational houses, and learning that way—the best way—by looking.

Of course we live in a world saturated by images; there are so many choices, so many ideas. So I hesitated to add more imagery to the mass of source material that already exists, but these houses reflect a way of putting together rooms that I hope is calmer, more subtle, slower and less frantic; an approach to decoration that is unhurried and personal, which is a true defining characteristic of the finest English interiors.

With this book, I have been fortunate to persuade ten good friends to open their doors to us, which is often a more daunting thing for them than you would imagine. However much I might tell someone that I think his or her house is beautiful, there is still trepidation in showing yourself to the world, not least because many of these friends are coincidentally some of the most modest and retiring people I know. And this is why we are luckier still. Over the course of a year now, Jan Baldwin has photographed these beautiful places; and, little by little, themes and variations emerge. I hope that you will enjoy the strands that tie these richly varied houses and interiors together, as well as looking at each in turn. Each brings its own contribution to a delicious feast of English decoration. Some are plain and nourishing, like Edward and Jane Hurst's serene kitchen opposite; some are like a delicate sorbet and others like a rich, comforting treacle pudding. All are in their way special to me, but not just as interiors. It is because they talk to me of friendship and of people. And this, ultimately, is why I love every house in this book. They are living, breathing places, overflowing with complexity and personality and stories. And that, in decoration, is the most magical and elusive quality of all.

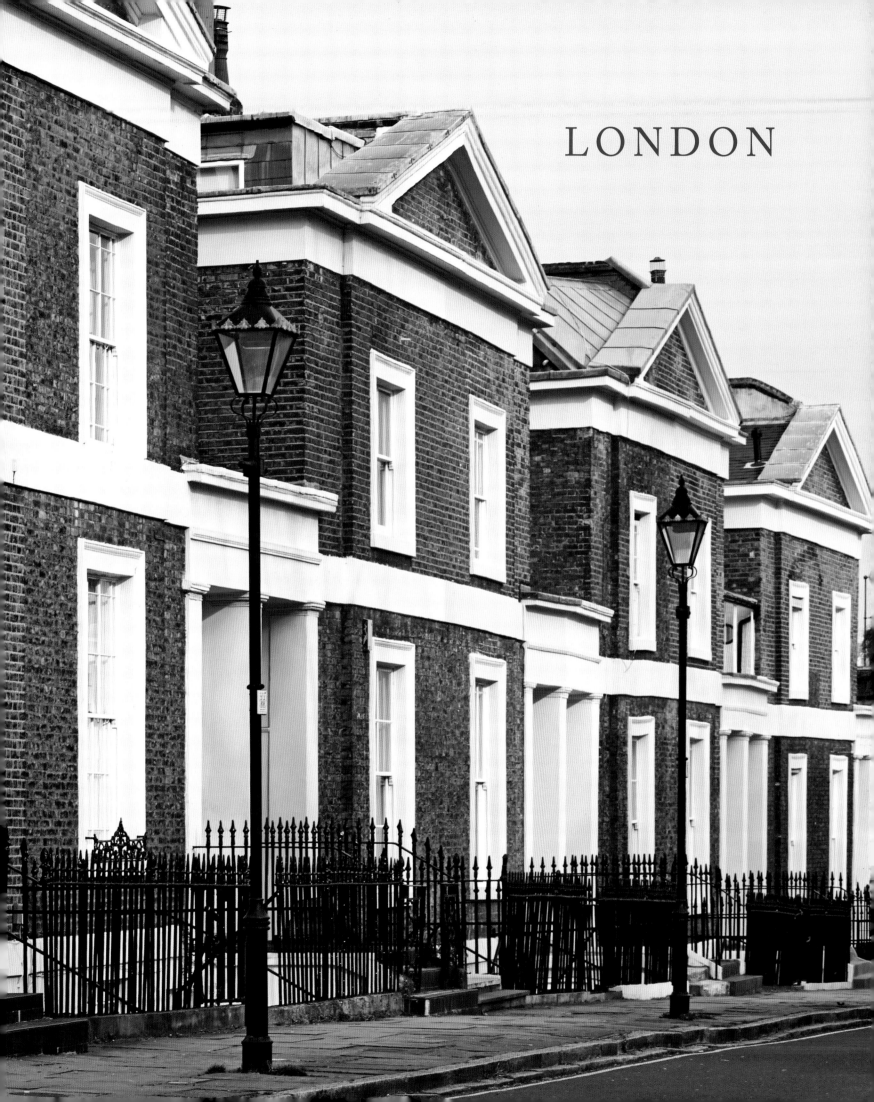

LONDON

Queen Square

A ROOFTOP FLAT IN BLOOMSBURY

Charlie and I live above the trees in an ancient, leafy London square. Our flat is on the top floor of a venerable artistic institution, the Art Workers' Guild, founded in the 1880s by followers of William Morris. In 1914, the Guild moved to this tall, rambling, early Georgian house in Queen Square, in the heart of Bloomsbury—now largely the preserve of hospitals and institutions. On cold winter evenings, ours are often the only lights glowing in the dark, silent square.

It is a beautiful building dating to about 1720, but our flat has little of the Georgian about it. When the Guild took over the house, they converted the upper floors into apartments, and instead of tiny attic windows for servants' rooms, we have a broad set of French doors facing east over the square. In the morning, the sun streams in. In the summer, we can throw open these doors and stand overlooking the treetops—and imagine that we are in Copenhagen or bohemian New York. London sometimes feels far away.

I like to approach the decoration of any house by first letting the building speak. We then introduce our own hopes and desires into the mix. Our Dorset house, which appears later in this book (see pages 78–95), is all about soft and faded English calm. Here in London, the volume is turned up a little. We both love colour and pattern, and against a simple backdrop of grey grasscloth walls and neutral, slubby furniture, I've introduced dashes of intense colour and print designed to make the eyes pop. The shifting collection of vibrant cushions speaks not only of colour clashes, but also of trips to Stockholm, Paris and New York. (I always think a cushion makes the nicest souvenir, and is by far the easiest to pack for the journey home.)

On the end wall of our sitting room is a strangely mottled stone fireplace, with an elaborate black japanned surround. It's a curiosity, and I can only imagine that, when the Art Workers' Guild was creating the flat in the 1920s, the piece was rejected from a Mayfair dressing room by a titled lady who had commissioned one of the distinguished architects that formed part of the Guild in those days. Somehow it doesn't quite belong. Whatever its actual history, it is a beautiful and unusual thing, rich and slightly exotic.

Immediately adjacent is a Fornasetti Palladiana chest of drawers; on the opposite wall hangs an entire framed set of John Rocque's famous 'Plan of the Cities of London, Westminster and Southwark' (which, I'm happy to say, we now sell in my shop, Pentreath & Hall). People visiting the flat for the first time can be absorbed for hours searching through the ancient streets and squares of Georgian London. Queen Square, of course, was laid out in the 1720s and is on Rocque's map, and we are reminded of the long palimpsest of history that makes up this wonderful, slightly forgotten corner of London.

Rich colours abound here. The kitchen is a sludgy brown-green, which a friend once disparagingly described as 'akin to the colour of a freshly laid cow pat'. I adore it (our bedroom in Dorset is painted exactly the same shade, and I use it again and again in our decoration projects). It is a colour from the 1950s range of paints by the great London colourman Patrick Baty. Sharp tones of yellow and orange enliven the room, and a couple of years ago I decided for some reason to paint the kitchen floor a pale gloss pink (it had been a neutral pale grey). It shouldn't work, but somehow everything hangs together. Next door, the stairwell is an olive green, also from Patrick's 1950s range—a brilliant colour against which to hang an eclectic collection of prints and photographs.

Two years ago I met my husband, Charlie McCormick. The relationship brought about a huge change in my life, but one that felt simultaneously intensely happy and completely inevitable. There have been changes. Here in London, and in Dorset, our homes have come to life because of it. Piles of books, clutter, little notes, postcards tucked on the mantelpiece; all signs that it is not just me at home now. When Charlie moved in, one of the first things we did was to redecorate the bedroom, and he picked a fresh bottle-green trellis wallpaper designed by our friend Lulu Lytle of Soane Britain (see pages 46–61), who introduced the two of us, no less. The room sparkles with colour in the afternoon light.

Charlie's chief joy is flowers, and the flat is never empty of blooms. Every week during the summer, he drives up from Dorset with bucketloads of flowers from the garden: dahlias, roses, sweet peas, peonies and nasturtiums. In winter, he makes perishingly cold early morning trips to New Covent Garden Market, returning well before dawn. And so our roof garden in London, which I started but then had neither the time nor energy to nurture, is now productive again, with large planted boxes of potatoes, peas, beans, herbs and salads burgeoning all summer long. The house has never felt so alive.

THE MAP WALL

Page 14 This framed map of John Rocque's 'Plan of the Cities of London, Westminster and Southwark' hung in my office for years. Each sheet of the map is close framed, so that the whole ties together to reveal mid-eighteenth-century London in fascinating detail. When I took on the flat, I realized one day that the end wall of the sitting room was almost the same dimension as the map. Several measurements later, it hangs in place—fitting perfectly.

THE GUEST BEDROOM

Page 17 In our tiny guest bedroom, the walls are papered in William Morris's Willow Bough, a wallpaper that I love and use time and again in our decoration projects. Above the little oak chest of drawers I've hung an ebonised Aesthetic Movement mirrored shelf of the same period as the wallpaper. It's home to a pair of brightly coloured china dogs by Rob Ryan that watch over everything and give a mildly contemporary edge to the room.

THE SITTING ROOM

Pages 18–19 The south wall of our sitting room glows with colour, although the main ingredients of the room—grasscloth walls, Beni Ourain rug, charcoal-grey linen sofa and Fornasetti chest—are all in their way quite neutral, drawing inspiration from the black japanned fire surround. Injections of colour come from the green Pentreath & Hall Library chair, cushions, a coral-red ottoman and piles of books. Textiles by Josef Frank add colour to the chair in the foreground, and a stripe by Madeleine Castaing makes a bold curtain.

SITTING-ROOM DETAILS

Page 20 More cushions add dashes of colour to the mid-century Danish sofa. Beyond is our dining table, also Danish 1960s, on which we have amassed too many pairs of silver column candlesticks—something I just can't stop buying. *Page 21* A bold ikat shade by Melodi Horne on a Pentreath & Hall lamp; the fern prints are nineteenth century; and the photographs are by James Ravilious, the son of Eric Ravilious, who designed the Coronation mug in the foreground.

MORE DETAILS

Page 22 A detail of our beautiful, curious, mottled-stone fireplace, with its Regency metal grate and unusual black japanned surround. The pattern perfectly relates to the mottled-brown glaze of an old Victorian mug.

Page 23 The hallway reveals a few of my passions: maps—this one, bought in New York, showing the southern tip of Manhattan; an ikat shade on a resin lamp by Marianna Kennedy; Hogarth prints (these are tea-stained photocopies stuffed into old frames); and books on type and typography.

THE KITCHEN AND HALLWAY

Page 24 The kitchen and hallway are next door to each other and painted two shades of dark sludgy green. The rooms are filled with splashes of bold colour— yellow blinds and lampshades, bright red chairs, and orange Le Creuset pots.

Page 25 Looking down the bedroom hallway. The walls are dark chocolate, hung with plasters by Peter Hone and crammed with pictures and books. Decoration transforms a narrow space into something unusual and interesting.

THE BATHROOM AND BEDROOM

Page 26 The bathroom is wallpapered in a moody, leafy grisaille paper, Richmond Park by Zoffany. The room is tiny and this bold three-dimensional paper gives it presence, but the pictures stop it becoming overwhelming.

Page 27 Our bedroom is papered in Seaweed Lace by Soane Britain, designed by Lulu Lytle (see pages 46–61). A Marianna Kennedy lamp with a blue shade, books and a bunch of fresh flowers make everything feel at home.

THE GUEST BEDROOM AND THE TERRACE

Page 28 The minuscule guest bedroom is given character by the cast-iron bed, painted in Charlotte's Locks by Farrow & Ball. I bought the bright yellow blanket at Svenskt Tenn in Stockholm. The door leads to our terrace garden.

Page 29 Amongst the chimneypots and rooftops of Bloomsbury is our roof terrace, which Charlie has filled with flowers and trees. On an upper level, the vegetable garden produces salads, herbs and flowers all summer.

Wharton Street

BURSTING WITH COLOUR IN KINGS CROSS

Tucked away between Bloomsbury and Islington, set back from the roar of Rosebery Avenue and the thundering traffic of Kings Cross Road, is a series of beautiful Regency streets where the houses are nicely-but-not-too-done-up, despite looming development all around. They have a settled air of gentle decay, as if their owners are confident enough not to need giant stainless-steel house numbers bolted to the door or on acid-etched fanlights to announce that they have moved in and taken over.

We are in the Lloyd Baker estate, perhaps the most distinctive of all the early nineteenth-century smaller London estates, with streets of 1820s paired Greek Revival villas 'dutifully climbing Lloyd Baker Street, two by two', as the architectural writer Ian Nairn put it so well in *Nairn's London*. Each duo is tucked neatly under a single, wide, low pediment whose architectural mouldings are drawn directly from the temples of Ancient Greece.

In the height of summer the house lived in by Maisie Rowe, and her twins Moss and Vera, is announced to the casual passer-by with a riotous fanfare of a front garden, from which bright orange marigolds and vivid pink lychnis spill out over the pavement. It is like a house from a children's book that wears a permanently happy smile on its face, and with a generous front door that beckons you in with a wide-armed hug.

Maisie is by profession a landscape architect, with a particular expertise in the landscape of play as experienced from the child's perspective, but she turns her talents to everything from accordion playing to decoration and gardening with equal zest—all with a delight in the sheer zaniness of life. It is a characteristic that infuses the house from top to toe.

The Lloyd Baker houses are not large. In a sense, they are barely more than cottages wearing a smart façade of grey brick and white stucco. There are two small and nicely proportioned rooms on the raised ground floor, two rooms on the first, and a little attic tucked into the eaves. Two flights down is the old kitchen in the basement, with doors leading to the garden. Perhaps it is this modest scale that gives us the feeling that we have stepped into a doll's house, but in this case, hinging open the demure brick front, we find it is owned by a child with a penchant for colour, pattern, enamel, flowers and plastic goods in bucketloads—and is humming throughout with humour. Spending a Sunday here, with Maisie and the children and friends, eating an enormous lunch, then playing upstairs with Moss and Vera all afternoon, is about the most contented way that Charlie and I know to spend a weekend in London—although not the quietest.

The house is as settled as a comfortable old slipper. You wouldn't have a clue that when Maisie first saw the house it was a wreck that needed almost total reconstruction. She understands exactly when to make changes, but also exactly when to stop. Who else would have retained the beautiful plywood kitchen designed by a former occupant, the architect Stephen Mullen, in the 1970s? In so many London houses today, such artefacts are mercilessly ripped out and replaced with sleek white German boxes or Shaker-style kitchens that are so tasteful

as to be utterly dull, ceilings filled with a landing-strip array of directional spotlights. Maisie has added to the kitchen, but has made her changes sympathetically. The cooking is still done on Stephen Mullen's lipstick-red AGA or on Maisie's vintage gas stove. Plates, bottles, saucepans and colanders hang from hooks or rest upon heaving shelves. The whole effect is one of happy chaos.

Another riot is happening on the ground floor, where the front sitting room is as unlike a traditional formal parlour as you can imagine. A burgeoning collection of multicoloured cushions spills, literally, over the edge of a deep sofa; above is an old bottle-drying rack that is home now to bunches of bright fake flowers (a mere echo of what grows in the garden all summer). It's a psychedelic experience: a 1970s children's picture book, a bonkers Indian restaurant and a Karma Cab all rolled into one.

The upstairs rooms are quieter but no less playful. Wallpapers by Cole and Son in Moss and Vera's bedrooms could be dull and grown up, but they are worn with a wink and a nod that brings a smile to your face. I don't know anyone else whose magnetic soap-holder is an elegant outstretched plastic hand, or who can get away with a blue plastic mirror above a 1960s turquoise-blue washbasin in the bathroom, without in any way looking cheap or tasteless. This is Maisie's unique skill. There's an Englishness to these interiors, but one that is infused with an enthusiasm for life that is surely global in its reach.

THE SITTING ROOM

Page 32 Above a huge Conran sofa overflowing with a rainbow-hued assortment of cushions, Maisie Rowe has hung an old bottle-drying rack filled with a vast array of fake flowers in the brightest neon colours imaginable. Not what you would expect to see on the wall of a sedate Regency townhouse, but all the more perfect for it. The walls are painted in a pale, chalky grey, specially mixed by Bridie Hall, with whom I now own our shop—it was Maisie who introduced us all those years ago.

THE KITCHEN WINDOW

Page 35 The lower-ground floors of Wharton Street are at garden level, with the street nearly a whole storey above. So we are looking here through the kitchen window to the old areaway and at a door into the coal cellar. But the room is not dark; it feels warm and cosy—as you will see on the following page. Maisie cooks on her vintage gas stove; an old set of slate-topped shelves is filled with a beautiful collection of bowls.

THE KITCHEN

Pages 36–37 I love Maisie's simple kitchen, installed by the previous owner, architect Steven Mullen, in the 1970s. The cherry-red AGA keeps the room toasty warm and meets its match in Maisie's extensive collection of coloured enamelware, hanging from many shelves. A Sheila Maid is suspended above, for drying laundry. Note the beautifully detailed joinery at the arch to the family room next door, original to the house.

INTERESTING CORNERS

Pages 38–39 Maisie is an inveterate collector and gatherer, a trait inherited in double measure by her twins, Moss and Vera. Bookshelves line a landing wall; mantelshelves are filled with collections of tiny model people and framed photographs; and a desk in the sitting room contains Maisie's collection of accordions. She is a renowned accordion player (playing beautifully at Charlie's and my wedding). I was shocked to see that Maisie won only second prize in the 'Garden in Bloom' competition, but such is the unfairness of life.

BEDROOMS AND BATHROOMS

Pages 40–41 The upstairs rooms are put together with a nonchalantly casual air that seems effortless. There are Cole and Son wallpapers in Vera and Moss's bedrooms; an old cast-iron bathtub is tucked into the eaves of the old attic, the walls scraped back but never repainted. Maisie has a simple four-poster bed in her bedroom, and she bought this beautiful Aesthetic Movement bamboo wardrobe for a song. The mother-of-pearl inlaid chair and table were inherited.

THE STREET

Page 42 On the first floor, Moss's bedroom overlooks the street and the colours of autumn leaves are reflected in the brilliant orange-yellow glow of his bed, beautifully painted in gloss, like much of the joinery at Wharton Street. Trunks and baskets are used for storage; plain linen curtains hang from a brass rod.
Page 43 Outside, in an autumnal dusk, are the villas of Wharton Street, 'climbing…two by two' under their paired Greek-Revival pediments.

Cleveland Square

THE CALL OF THE EAST IN WEST LONDON

Lulu Lytle is one of the brightest lights in the London design world, and her shop Soane Britain is uncontestably the leading champion of British-made furniture, fabric, wallpaper and lighting. Since 1997, when Lulu (then in partnership with that doyen of English decoration Christopher Hodsoll) first opened her doors on London's Pimlico Road, flanked by venerable antiques dealers, she has developed a collection of furniture and furnishings of extraordinary distinction and complexity—and all of it made in Britain.

How rare is this today? Here we find the work of English metalworkers and woodcarvers, of leatherworkers and cabinetmakers, of old textile mills and wallpaper-printing studios, and, most recently, of rattan weavers—Soane rescued from extinction the very last English rattan workshop, threatened with closure, five years ago. There is a touch of romantic persuasion to Lulu Lytle's mission that is not attuned to that harsh-minded world of business, driven purely by the bottom line, which seeks to outsource wherever it goes. Yet it works. As I am writing, Lulu—whose energy knows few bounds—has just opened her first New York showroom. Over her shop doors could be inscribed John Ruskin's famous statement: *'There is hardly anything in the world that someone cannot make a little worse and sell a little cheaper, and those who consider price alone are that man's lawful prey.'* A sentiment, I suspect, with which many readers of this book will agree.

Lulu's style drinks deeply from tradition but is never imitative or dull. Her great influence is Peter Twining, the crème of London antiques dealers, the ultimate aesthete, and the first to make startling design statements such as the juxtaposition of an Irish eighteenth-century side table with a Japanese bronze and 1930s lighting. So it is no surprise that the generous West London apartment that Lulu and her husband Charlie have made their home for seventeen years is one of the most beautiful and interesting you are likely to see.

We are on the top floor of a massive, late nineteenth-century house on Cleveland Square, in a terrace of cream-painted stucco, one of those giant wedding-cake, many-columned mansions built for the Victorian upper classes. Cleveland Square is green and leafy and asymmetrical, with a confusing one-way system that is the bane of taxi drivers and occasional visitors like myself. (The confusion was intentionally planned, Lulu tells me, to frustrate the trade of prostitutes from nearby Paddington Station.)

Lulu and Charlie's apartment is on the upper floor of this building, once the servants' bedrooms, and spreads laterally over three of the houses. So the views, over private gardens, are beautiful—but the ceilings are low. They gutted and reconstructed the flat to create a huge yet homely space; it has a restraint, a modesty, about it that combines with Lulu's assured skills as an interior decorator and furniture designer to make a place that feels like few I know in London. It is quietly glamorous, yet settled, relaxed and comfortable all at the same time.

The *pièce de résistance* is the fine drawing room, facing south over the private gardens; a room seemingly purpose-made for entertaining, for drinking cocktails by the light of a blazing fire, for conversation on deep and embracing sofas or at the card table, reflected in the light of mirrored walls that extend the envelope of this room to infinity.

Who else but Lulu would place an enormous royal-blue zigzag carpet across the floor or paint the ceiling duck-egg grey? This is unconventional decoration with a kick, and the room delivers a shot of energy to the soul. We encounter Lulu's love of extraordinary prints and paintings of animals—a blue-nosed baboon in a lipstick-red frame, a prowling tiger and a watercolour of a giant rhinoceros. Elsewhere, there are lions, camels, giraffes and hares. Her other great passion is books. The room is shelved at both ends, groaning with an enviable collection of art,

decoration and furniture books. (If you visit Lulu's office at Soane, tucked into the attics, you can hardly see her desk underneath the overflowing piles of books and old auction catalogues. Every time I see her there, she pretends that she is clearing catalogues out of her life, but I suspect this task is rather like cleaning the Augean stables—it will never be completed.)

Here and there, of course, are moments of gentleness. Lulu and Charlie's bedroom is calm and soothing; and which young girl wouldn't want Bunny Lytle's beautiful bed, tented in Soane's Raspberry Ripple Stripe? But the entire apartment is infused with colourful tones of the East—appropriately, perhaps, for a former student of Egyptology and Ancient History.

The richly toned snug is the epicentre of this orientalist dream: the pink walls hung with a narwhal tusk, textiles and prints, and paintings of Ottoman Turks and Arabian warriors, while models of minarets and Persian ceramics rest between ikat lampshades and beaten-brass vessels. The whole is carried off perfectly and the recipe given added zest by a pair of Soane fireside chairs upholstered in the jewel-like hues of Lulu's Damascus Stripe silk. Curiously, I am most jealous of the collection of framed nineteenth-century photographs of Egypt that line the walls of the guest lavatory, gently glazed in golden brown.

There is further use of rich colour in the kitchen, with its wall of turquoise glazed tiles. This is a wonderful room, the heart of the flat, around which dinner parties last long into the night. It was at this table that I met my husband Charlie, so it will hold a special place in my heart for ever. Eating delicious dinners by candlelight here, with vivacious conversation flowing around the table, reminds one of the generosity, friendliness and brilliant humour that is at the centre of this home—qualities that are ultimately far more important than even the most beautiful decoration.

THE DEN, DETAIL

Page 46 A study in tones of pink: a corner of the family's favourite room in the house, the Den, with its boldly hued walls. The nineteeth-century Syrian inlaid demi-lune table is one of Lulu's favourites; a blue-and-white vase contains English roses grown by Bridget Elworthy at Wardington (see pages 148–167), and a nineteenth-century Turkish turban incenser has a beautiful profile. The wallhanging is eighteenth-century Greek and inspired a Soane fabric, Symi.

THE DEN FIREPLACE

Page 49 Lulu lined the fireplace with turquoise-blue tiles bought in Morocco and finished it with a brass trim. In this cosiest corner of the house, a pair of slipper chairs by the fire are upholstered in Soane's jewel-toned Damascus Stripe. Above hangs a nineteenth-century painting of a Turkish soldier known as a bashi-bazouk. To the right is a brass Tibetan trumpet, which Lulu has yet to learn to play; the wooden lion was found in Portobello Road market.

THE DEN

Pages 50–51 A deeply comfortable Bunny sofa, made by Soane Britain and named after Lulu's eldest daughter, is upholstered in a Rubelli Suzani. With its shades of rose red and carmine and flashes of blue, it was the old striped kelim, bought from Peter Hinwood, which provided the inspiration for the room. The wall paint was specially mixed by Rose Dailey. Soane's Raspberry Paw Print fabric has been used to cover the foreground chair and make the curtains. It's hard to imagine a nicer place to curl up on a Sunday afternoon.

THE KITCHEN

Pages 52–53 When Lulu and Charlie first moved into the flat, they knocked out the walls of three rooms to make a wide, welcoming kitchen. They installed oak cabinets and a copper-wrapped island that have stood the test of time (like fixtures in all the best kitchens). The walls are lined in turquoise glazed tiles from World's End Tiles (now, sadly, discontinued); a copper Owl lantern from Soane Britain hangs above the dining table, with its set of beautiful, battered leather Soane Casino dining chairs—an iconic and timeless design.

THE BLUE ROOM

Pages 54–55 This sophisticated, sensual room is given scale by the blue carpet with huge zigzags, designed by Lulu and Peter Twining and woven by Veedon Fleece. Peter advised covering the walls in plate-glass mirrors with bevelled edges, so that the room dissolves and expands to infinity. Lulu had the mirror drilled to accommodate picture hooks. Soane Bergère chairs and a card table make a comfortable spot by the fireplace, with its simple surround designed by Peter in golden glowing Syrian marble.

THE BEDROOMS

Page 56 A nineteenth-century satinwood wardrobe adds warmth to Lulu and Charlie's bedroom, where the walls are painted a putty colour. The silk-upholstered slipper chair is from Soane; textiles, hangings and an old Turkey rug on the floor give the room a cosy, quiet atmosphere at night.
Page 57 Enclosing Bunny's bed with hangings in Soane's Ripple Stripe is a wonderful touch in a friendly room, enlivened by pictures and photos and a Tulu rug. Bunny's favourite teddy, Rabby, sits comfortably on the pillow.

THE BATHROOM, CLOAKROOM AND LAUNDRY

Pages 58–59 Lulu decided to have an imitiation lapis-lazuli basin top and mirror, made in cast scagliola, which requires oiling three times a week to retain its lustre. It is an eye-catching detail in her splendid bathroom. The cloakroom is painted by Rose Dailey and lined with photographs of Egyptian temples; in the hall is a cast of a *Sivatherium Giganteum* (a prehistoric giraffe from the Himalayas). Above the laundry hangs an old Suffolk butcher's sign; of all Lulu's extraordinary possessions, this is perhaps the one I most covet.

Jermyn Street

ST. JAMES'S CLASSICAL REINVENTED

Kim Wilkie is happiest spending a day on the farm with his Longhorn cattle, some of the most cosseted and contented animals on earth, or cutting the low-growth branches from his maturing acres of woodland. Kim is perhaps the leading landscape architect of his generation, with an incisive understanding of what is right for a place. I am fortunate enough to have worked with him on many projects and we have become great friends.

Kim's skills are in demand around the world, meaning that he cannot entirely bury himself in the narrow hidden lanes of Hampshire. Three years ago, he realized that life would be transformed by finding a small pied-à-terre in the heart of London. After a lot of looking, he discovered the dream flat in a mansion block in St. James's, on the upper floor of a distinguished Portland stone building dating from the late nineteenth century, complete with fluted Doric columns as correctly disposed as a tightly furled city umbrella.

This area of London, bordering Piccadilly, is one part gentleman's clubland, one part epicentre of British tailoring, and one part the hushed heart of the softly carpeted, softly lit St. James's art world. All of these characteristics are so far from Kim's natural habitat that I was at first surprised to hear he had found his perch on Jermyn Street. It would be impossible to imagine Kim, the gentlest and one of the most relaxed people I know, wearing a tightly buttoned Jermyn Street shirt or silk tie, yet this little nook that he has made his own in the heart of London is perfect for him. If we remember that we are also near Green Park and Burlington House, the home of the Royal Academy of Arts, it is not hard to appreciate that Kim is secretly quite pleased to get his groceries from Fortnum & Mason (the smartest corner shop in the world).

Kim's flat had last been done up in the 1980s, for an elderly couple, and was resplendent with dragged walls and ruched blinds. There was a pair of enormous pink sofas left behind, which needed to be chopped up to get them through the door. The conversion had been done poorly, with badly laid-out rooms and falling-to-bits kitchen and bathrooms, but the building had tall ceilings and large windows, and he knew that something special could be made here. It was time to make a clean sweep.

Kim hired our mutual friend William Smalley to do the job. William is a London-based architect who has developed his own distinctive design language, which rests somewhere between a profound reverence for tradition and an uncompromising minimalism. It is hard to define William's work without using the hackneyed expression timeless, but maybe the better word is private. Nothing here is ostentatious. There is an inner modesty that suits Kim like a glove. The project was a perfect collaboration.

Everything is deeply considered, but rarely designed to within an inch of its life. William's schemes contain serious thought, but they wear it lightly, almost nonchalantly—which is why I identify them as quintessentially English. You will not find here the cluttered, squashy-sofa school of comfort of the typical English interior, but something of a different sort—the comfort that derives from knowing that everything works and is quietly harmonious. It is the comfort of simplicity, a quality that is often evident in the cool, limewashed walls of a medieval building, which has been filtered and made lucid through a completely modern sensibility.

A diminutive front door opens to a vaulted hallway; symmetrical doors to left and right lead to the study, guest bathroom, kitchen and to a main, tall-ceilinged living room that has three huge windows facing south over Jermyn Street. Beyond is the bedroom, which faces a quiet, airy courtyard lined with white glazed tiles. All the walls and joinery are painted a particular shade of white from Mylands of London; floors are in wide-planked oak, the skirting boards are tall and, like all the joinery, were custom-designed and made for their rooms. The kitchen, from Bulthaup, is pure white and stainless steel. If empty, the apartment would be as serene and quiet as a monastery. Visiting on a hot afternoon in the height of summer is like entering a cool temple.

Into this world Kim has brought his happy, friendly magic. At the Hampshire farm that he shares with his partner Pip Morrison (himself a brilliant landscape architect), the language is one of oak beams and ancient, polished furniture and carefully chosen pieces of glass and china. There are deep, comfortable sofas, rich colours, and giant pots of sweetly scented flowers brought in from the glasshouse. Something of this quality infuses the St. James's apartment, which goes to show how much more important the occupation of a house is than its structure. Here is a warmth and richness that comes from comfortable pieces of furniture, Arts and Crafts oak, Georgian mahogany, or contemporary Perspex, put together with the confident eye of someone who respects the process and the making as much as the result. Pictures, framed posters, and textiles have meaning and memory, and perhaps my favourite piece of all is Kim's ancient battered trunk—a family heirloom, testament to the Wilkies' diplomatic days.

Ancient meets modern throughout. On the wall to the right of the fireplace are thirty-five beautiful ploughshares, dug by Kim and Pip from the fields of their farm, now brought to London and displayed with a sculptural beauty that would not look out of place in the gallery of a dealer of the finest mid-century art, a few short steps away. Life has a strange and appropriate way of turning full circle.

THE STUDY FIREPLACE

Page 62 The nineteenth-century fireplace is original to the flat. Its marble shelf is the surface for an ephemeral collection: a fine Victorian church candlestick, beautifully polished; a pair of green glass trumpet vases; a model of Kim's scheme for the surroundings of London's Natural History Museum, where he is completely reworking the approach to Waterhouse's great building; and some postcards, one of which is from me—a watercolour of the little church at Profiti Ilias on the Greek island of Patmos.

A SITTING-ROOM DETAIL

Page 65 A vase and dish in Kim's sitting room were made by Peter Beard, a distinguished ceramicist, metalworker and stonecarver based in Warwickshire, where he creates these luminescent vessels in shades of turquoise, blue and grey. Their colours make a harmonious complement to a bunch of blue and white anemones. Beneath this ensemble is Kim's ancient black trunk, marked many times with the name Wilkie and used by several generations of diplomats in the family.

THE SITTING ROOM AND KITCHEN

Pages 66–67 William Smalley designed the sitting room to be stripped of all detail, except for a tall skirting board and a wide-planked oak floor. Together, he and Kim designed the stone fire surround in polished Purbeck marble. The sofa is from Viaduct, the coral-red kelim is from the Conran shop, and the dining table and chairs are by Ambrose Heal. Above the dining table hangs a painted map of London by Barbara Macfarlane; above the sofa is a monoprint by Julian Meredith. The simple kitchen is by Bulthaup.

STUDY AND SITTING-ROOM DETAILS

Page 68 Kim's study has a glass table on an oak frame from Conran and an Italian Perspex desk chair from the 1970s. Above a handsome Welsh oak cupboard is a framed drawing of Kim's masterplan for the western reaches of the Thames Landscape Strategy, from Hampton to Kew.

Page 69 In the sitting room, above a Heal's chest of drawers, is another remarkable landscape drawing—Charles Bridgeman's plan for Stowe in Buckinghamshire. In front are two burnished bowls by Duncan Ross.

THE STUDY

Pages 70–71 The pair of large windows in Kim's study looks out on Jermyn Street. He has placed his desk beside them to make the most of the light. This is a peaceful and lovely room to work in. Above the sofa hang some of Kim's own photographs of his landscapes; on the opposite wall, above the fireplace, is a drawing by John Coker. When there is no one else in the flat, the only thing to interrupt the silence is the slow, resonant tick of the grandfather clock, which Kim inherited.

THE BATHROOM AND BEDROOM

Pages 72–73 A Heal's bed and Owl chest of drawers bring a friendly humour to the bedroom. Old rugs add cosiness and texture to the space. The Ovale bathtub is from Holloways of Ludlow; above it hangs a picture by Janice Gray, and tall church candles illuminate the room at night. In the passage leading to the bedroom, William designed plain oak shelves to house Kim's collection of ancient ploughshares, dug from the fields of Kim and Pip's Hampshire farm.

COUNTRY

The Old Parsonage

DORSET REGENCY REVISITED

If you are familiar with my previous book, *English Decoration*, and are the sort of person who likes playing spot the difference, then you will enjoy this chapter. For we are now back at my home in West Dorset, the place that has been, I sometimes feel, the making of me, as well as providing the balm to my life for the past eight years: this is the place that I come to get away from it all. It's amazing to think that I've lived here for almost a decade; time rushes by, but in one sense, it feels far longer than this, too. It is a wonderful thing to begin to be rooted to a spot, to see a house and garden develop season after season.

There are obvious changes that the sharp-eyed will spot—new paint colours, new acquisitions, pictures and furniture that have moved around—but there is one great, incredible change: my husband, Charlie McCormick. When we were introduced around Lulu Lytle's dining table (see page 52), who would have imagined that a year later we would be married? One of the things that has made me happiest of all is the way in which Charlie has made the Parsonage his own; both in the garden, where he is in the midst of creating an extraordinary work of art that is scented, multi-textured, richly coloured, and in the house, which has never felt so friendly and alive.

The Parsonage has been transformed by becoming a shared place, and the truth is that without this transformation I suspect that by now I would have been ready to move on. My interest in the creative aspect—restoring the house, reviving the garden—had inevitably waned with time (I am always in search of a new project rather than enjoying the fruit of my labours). But Charlie has turned the house into our home, the place we both want to be all the time; and it makes me realize (as if we didn't already know it) that the qualities that make a building feel loved, generous and welcoming are more to do with people than with architecture or decoration. It is a powerful lesson.

The house is Regency, built in the 1820s, with all the simple plain elegance of that moment in English architecture. There were a few changes and extensions a couple of decades later, but the building was virtually untouched thereafter. On its own, the house would be unremarkable, but it stands in an idyllic position on a south-facing slope in one of the most beautiful small villages in Dorset, looking across a valley to wooded hills opposite. The position is dreamlike, and gives this otherwise humble place a sense of light and perspective that is breathtaking. There is a wide, south-facing elevation with three bays, and a smaller, two-bay façade facing west over the lawn and flower borders, to which I added a little timber-trellised porch around the garden door.

Inside, it is three-up, three-down, with a child's small bedroom in the attic. When I first settled in, the rooms were spare and uncluttered. I thought about, but was slightly wary of, introducing colour; I painted the walls in shades of white, softest grey and stone. The house in those days had a lucidity that was very calm and tranquil, but if I am honest it could feel a little chilly during long, cold Dorset winters. So as I settled in, and as the years passed and the rooms filled with clutter and the walls with pictures, I became more adventurous in the use of colour— with the advantage of being able to live with great patches of colour on the walls before making final commitments. It is much easier to do this in a furnished room, living with thoughts through different lights and seasons, than walking into an empty space and immediately making choices.

So you can spy rooms in my previous book that have now changed. The kitchen, once white, is now a dark burnt orange; the drawing room, previously pale grey, is a soft warm pink, which I had specially mixed for the room, as I couldn't find exactly the right colour on a chart. Our bedroom is now a dark, sludgy colour that I adore—the same colour as our kitchen in London (see page 24). The dining room had a brief moment (recorded in a photograph or two) in an extraordinarily intense 1960s purple, Victoria Plum, which divided opinion strongly. It had a beauty by candlelight but was, to say the least, a difficult colour on a bright sunny day. Charlie hated it, quite rightly, so one of the first things we did was to repaint the room in the brightest cornflower blue, which is equally eye-popping but has the advantage of being a happy colour, rather than making you look very slightly ill.

Other changes are more subtle. It is reassuring to see, four years on, how little has changed in some areas. But even here we can sense clutter, accumulations, pieces of furniture squeezed in, even more piles of books, and, now, everywhere, many bunches of flowers from the beginning of spring to the dying days of autumn—Charlie is a brilliant and insatiable grower of cut flowers and there is never a moment when something is not brought in from garden to house, reinforcing that magical connection between building and setting with which I opened this chapter. As I write, there are plans afoot that we will be joined by a puppy, a kitten, several chickens and a rabbit. The Parsonage has never felt more like a home.

DINING-ROOM DETAIL

Page 78 Charlie and I recently repainted the dining room a bold cornflower blue, St. Giles Blue by Farrow & Ball. The engravings are by Piranesi, part of a growing collection that fills our walls here and in my office in London. The bright red chair is one of a set of Chinese bamboo chairs, made in the 1970s, which I bought from my friend and neighbour Anthony Sykes—a startling splash of colour against the walls. The lamp and shade are from my shop.

THE DINING ROOM

Page 81 More Piranesi above the sideboard, part of an extraordinary series depicting Roman funerary monuments and inscriptions. I adore their graphic quality. The sideboard is Regency, picked up for a song in a London auction; the table is substantial, nineteenth century, bought in Dorset, and I found the six oak dining chairs, also Victorian, on eBay. They have their original faded velvet covers. Charlie grows abundant old English roses in the garden.

THE DRAWING ROOM AND HALLWAY

Page 82 A corner of the drawing room shows the generous bay window, which is the perfect place for this Regency bamboo sofa. A Howard armchair is upholstered in a blue antique linen by Polly Lyster.
Page 83 A glimpse of the dining room and, reflected in the mirror, the front door with its pretty Regency fanlight. We bought the huge blue-and-white flowery jug, much mended, at Portobello Road market. The wallpaper is Malahide by David Skinner, based on a nineteenth-century original.

THE DRAWING ROOM

Pages 84–85 The drawing room has evolved since it was last photographed for *English Decoration*. There is more clutter now, with even more furniture and cushions, and I think the room is all the more comfortable for it. The walls are painted in specially mixed Parsonage Pink by Patrick Baty, against which the yellow linen sofa from my friend Max Rollitt sings brightly. After eight years of use, the Regency marble fireplace from Jamb is ageing gracefully.

THE KITCHEN

Pages 86–87 Again, evolution: when I first arrived here, I painted the walls white. A couple of years later, I needed a change and chose Farrow & Ball's Archive colour Wet Sand. The room was transformed at a stroke. Now we are thinking of a buttercup yellow. This is the least fitted kitchen I know, with a tall bank of old joinery to the right of the AGA, and a dresser that I bought on eBay. A sink, with dishwasher and washing machine, is behind us.

THE LANDING AND BEDROOMS

Pages 88–89 The rooms at the Parsonage are sunny and south-facing, with a view across the narrow wooded valley to hills beyond. The four-poster bed in the guest bedroom, which I inherited from my grandparents, was moved from London. The patchwork-quilt bedspread was made by my mother. Bedroom curtains are in Bowness, a document print by Jean Monro, or, in the other guest room, brown cotton ticking—an excellent choice for a simple cottage interior.

OUR BEDROOM

Pages 90–91 When I first arrived at the Parsonage, I painted this room a soft light grey. It was a lovely colour but I got bored with it. This velvety olive-brown is from Patrick Baty's 1950s range and is the same colour as our kitchen in London (see page 24). The Staffordshire dogs on the mantelpiece, with rare green colouring, were part of a group of about twenty that Charlie and I bought from a surprised antiques shop owner in Somerset last winter.

THE VEGETABLE GARDEN

Pages 92–93 In the height of summer, the vegetable garden reaches its ebullient green peak. I set out the garden when I first arrived here, lifting the lawn and laying new brick paths that aged in an instant. But the garden is now Charlie's domain, and he is brilliant at creating a lush abundance. You can see the Parsonage, built into the hillside of a valley, on the south-facing slope, with the humble Victorian church tucked just below.

On a Dorset Hillside

AN ARTIST'S FARM BY THE SEA

In the far west of Dorset, hidden in a deep valley, is one of the most beautiful houses I have known. It is the home of an artist, originally from Connecticut, who arrived with his wife in this remote spot some 45 years ago and never left. The house was an old dilapidated farm, the remains of a tiny hamlet that retains its own chapel, on a steeply sloping site facing east, with long views across the valley to the shining sea.

Here, they made a home, and have created over the decades a remarkable garden that defies belief. Coming here on a drowsy, midsummer evening, the air pregnant with the heavy scents of wisteria, iris, and old-fashioned roses, with foxgloves glowing pale apricot-white at dusk, it is like entering a garden of paradise. There are mown-grass paths tucked between tall hedges and tiny cobbled footpaths leading to enclosed garden rooms with seats and chairs; each leading to the next delight, all tumbling down the steep easterly-facing slope until you reach woods and open fields at the bottom. All around are softly rolling hills and the sound of sheep, and as night settles we could be in the Dorset of Thomas Hardy a hundred or more years ago. It is a dream house, in a dream landscape, and Charlie and I count ourselves lucky that this is the house of friends, who live just a few hills beyond us.

The owners are no longer young, but they retain a youthful vigour, a spark, that is inspirational. I hope that I might be like this in the future—settled, peaceful, contented, yet still working and creating hard (in the beautiful, light-filled artists' studio next door to the house), still gardening profusely. I believe that part of their vigour derives from the place, from the grey-walled, lichen-encrusted farmhouse surrounded by wide green fields, fresh air and clear blue sky, and from where, on a summer's day, you can see as far into the past, and into the future, as you may imagine.

The house has two parts, each with its own distinct character. To the south is the tall, three-storey, three-bay original house, with a wide front; it has stone-mullioned casement windows and a beautiful, restrained, classical door case bearing a date stone from 1786. To the north is a later wing, more cottage-like, which curiously feels earlier and doubtless incorporates—like so many Dorset farmhouses—earlier elements: ancient windows, an old gothic-arched door head, and rubble stone walls that feel as if they belonged to an older building at an earlier time. The cottage contains the entrance hall, pantry and low-ceilinged bedrooms. The main house has a kitchen, drawing room, sitting rooms and bedrooms with distant views across the Dorset country. The whole is a happy amalgam of eighteenth- and nineteenth-century bits; two staircases lead to the different parts, but in curious places upstairs the rooms connect, so that the house flows together as a seamless whole.

The place is famous for its sloping garden of many rooms, which (very rarely open to the public) is written about in reverential tones by the best garden writers; and it is, of course, a beautiful garden indeed. But the first time I went over to meet our artist and his wife, with mutual friends who were staying with me, there was a moment—as we crossed the threshold into the old farmhouse—when my eyes watered with delight. The interior of the farmhouse is a greater joy, perfect for being not too thought about, so utterly uncontrived; rooms just 'put together' and all the more heavenly for it.

There is a calm and unhurried air about these interiors that defies fashion or trend; it is the finest sort of English decoration, completely timeless, which has hardly changed or shifted over half a century of happy family life. William Morris wallpapers, currently enjoying a renaissance, were pasted to these ancient walls with the enthusiasm of the early 1970s, the decade that first discovered so many of the themes that press us now with new resonance—the need to understand craft, and the handmade; to know provenance, not just of old furniture, but of how new things are made, or where our food is grown and harvested. Curtains were made that have hung here for fifty years, gently fading in a way that is impossible to achieve except through time itself. Rugs were laid, chairs reupholstered, colours picked… the whole settled by the sunlight of decades and by the placidity of the place, yet as fresh as the day they were chosen.

There is a gentle sense of order to these rooms that feels deeply benign; everything finds its place. There is no ostentation; nothing is without interest, but nothing shouts. A restful quality extends across the whole house in a way that is soothing and quiet; qualities that can be found equally in the extraordinary oil paintings that have been produced over the decades next door, and which today find themselves hanging in important collections around the world. These same qualities extend from the house to the garden and back again. The house bears little frivolity; it has a feeling of calm seriousness, the seriousness of centuries of farm work, which has been succeeded for these past five decades by a different, but no less serious, job of work. Yet it is a happy place, with a sense of deep contentment, and this beautiful house slowly inhales and exhales, looked after and cherished by its owners, knowing that it will be as loved by the next generation as the current. It is my favourite sort of place.

THE COTTAGE

Page 96 An old gate opens to reveal a cobbled path to the front door of the north wing of the farmhouse, built in the nineteenth century, with a steep catslide roof coming down to the stone-mullioned windows. The garden is planted with a heady blend of English cottage garden flowers, and a wisteria clambers around the entrance. It is as if you are entering a completely secret garden, and you know that you are in a magical place.

THE RED ROOM

Page 99 In winter, this is the cosiest room in the house, leading both to the kitchen and to the conservatory shown on page 103. An old Victorian nursing chair catches the soft Dorset light. It is upholstered in the same beautiful fabric as the curtains, which was designed by David Bishop, who in the 1960s had a small shop on the King's Road selling Indian block-printed fabrics that became the basis for the first collection of Designers Guild fabrics when it opened in 1971. The lampshade was hand-painted by the owner.

THE HALLWAY

Pages 100–101 When the owners restored the farmhouse in the 1970s, they installed this lovely simple staircase in plain beaded board; the newel post has a gothic detail to match the little internal window. The joinery is painted a perfect primrose yellow. Comfortable clutter fills this room, and useful things: walking sticks and umbrellas, tennis balls for the dog, and a roll of twine. A mid-Georgian chest of drawers is home to a beautiful olive-green lamp, with a shade hand-painted by the owner.

THE GREEN ROOM AND CONSERVATORY

Page 102 In the older part of the house is this lovely sitting room, painted a rich leaf green. The mantelshelf is filled with clutter and mementos, including two unusual ceramic candlesticks bought in Marrakech in the 1970s. The brown and electric blue candles provide a perfect splash of colour. Bookshelves flank the chimney breast and bring warmth and texture to the room.
Page 103 The conservatory, tucked onto the south side of the house, overflows with planting, including a lush and productive vine.

THE KITCHEN

Pages 104–105 An old and beautifully proportioned country dresser is painted a beautiful teal blue, the walls are mustard yellow, and the AGA is bottle green: a rich and lovely palette that belongs perfectly in this old farmhouse. The dresser has the right mix of display and use; nothing is self-conscious in this room. The ceiling light was bought from Dennis Ray, in London, and painted by the owner. It is not everyone's cup of tea, but I love its zany exuberance.

THE BEDROOMS

Pages 106–107 The bedrooms are decorated with a calm and timeless quality. Soft colours and shades reflect those of the Dorset landscape: faded green, browns, pale blues and stone greys. Pattern abounds; small prints on bedspreads, chairs, curtains and wallpapers. The master bathroom is one of my favourite rooms, with a bathtub installed in the middle of the room, the walls papered in William Morris's classic Willow Bough (the dreamy hand-blocked version), and furnished like a dressing room.

THE DAIRY

Pages 108–109 Across the farmyard is a small, single-storey dairy that has been transformed into a beautiful cottage by the owners' daughter. The walls are tongue-and-groove boarding, which feels fresh and warm at the same time. The old stone walls of the building are painted white; the joinery is a mix of soft summery hues. Above the sofa in the sitting room is a landscape by the West Dorset artist Vanessa Gardiner. Below, Percy sits in his favourite spot.

THE HOUSE

Pages 110–111 A view from the fields, showing the old rubble stone walls of the farmhouse, beautifully coursed, and the fine Purbeck slate roof. Sheep graze peacefully and all is quiet in this remote, placid spot. Looking back at the farm, we see a view unchanged for two hundred years and which, we can feel sure, will remain unchanged three hundred years from now: England at her finest.

Manor Farmhouse

ANTIQUE HEAVEN IN NORTH DORSET

Anyone who has the pleasure of crossing the threshold of Edward and Jane Hurst's sublime, restrained house in Dorset will realize immediately that they are entering the home of a rare couple. Edward is the leading English antiques dealer of our generation, with an eye for the unusual that surpasses anyone else I know. He also acts as an interior consultant, weaving his spell across many houses now. Jane is a gardener, cook and potter of great skill; an artist in everything she touches. The combination of these two beautiful, quiet people—with the added zest of their horse-mad daughter Fleur and antiques-dealing son Tom (now 16, who started buying and selling at the age of nine)—is magical, and this place that they have made in their quiet corner of Dorset is close to heaven.

Once a farm, and surrounded still by handsome barns now used as stabling and to store some of Edward's larger pieces of furniture (and from time to time to throw grand dinners along trestle tables lined with dozens of chairs, lit only by candles), the house is of pale red brick and sits at the end of a long lane with the unusual name of Telegraph Street. Opposite, behind more brick garden walls, is the tempting architectural façade of the much grander manor house. It is a special corner of an unspoiled village.

But the real enchantment starts within. Colours, furniture, pictures, objects and the fruits of the garden combine to create one of the most beautiful sets of English domestic rural interiors imaginable. Everything is in harmony—still, calm, gentle, welcoming—and just right. Many of the pieces of furniture are of important provenance, destined for the stand that, once a year, Edward takes at the cream of London antiques fairs, Masterpiece. However, above all, this isn't a museum. It's a slightly chaotic, ever-so-slightly rambling family home, and that is why it feels so good to be here.

Edward's style matches his persona—quiet, unassuming, deeply English, imbued with a love for (and a deep knowledge of) history—all worn with a sparky irreverence that stops anything feeling dull. He is responsible for the house, Jane for the garden; a symbiotic relationship that has much to do with the calmness that fills the whole place.

No room in the farmhouse is large. An old low wing at the rear was enlarged in the early nineteenth century with a handsome new front, three storeys tall and two rooms deep, which I always think is looking at the world with an expression of startled surprise, not unlike Edward himself. Its rooms are square and well proportioned but modest in scale. The front door opens onto a long hall, recently tiled in black-and-white encaustic flooring. To the left is the drawing room, with French doors to the garden; and to the right, a dining room. Beyond is a small winter snug, perhaps my favourite room in the house, which leads to the tranquil kitchen in the old wing; a room that feels completely timeless, as if we have just stepped back into the early nineteenth century, with slate-flagged floors, a wide scrubbed table and a tall green cupboard that contains all pots, plates and food.

The drawing room is a quiet and serene space. It has its moment of fireworks in the startlingly beautiful japanned cabinet that stands to the left of the fireplace and the Dutch *tulipieres* on the mantelshelf, both surmounted by

dozens of dried allium heads that Jane saves each year from the garden. Velvets, needlepoint, and richly patterned Turkey rugs contrast with the plain linen upholstered chairs and sofa. From the French doors, steps lead up to Jane's wide garden borders, filled with plants that combine the best of classic English herbaceous planting with a modern Dutch sensibility. Stepping out of these doors on a warm summer evening for cocktails on the terrace before one of Jane's deliciously cooked dinners—the air heady with scent from potted flowers—is probably as close to perfect as you can find in the back lanes of North Dorset.

The dining room, by contrast, is a rich space, the walls covered with specially mixed paint of an extraordinary orange-red shade that by candlelight takes on a glowing intensity. Dinners around this table are long, happy, and full of conversation (and many a night here have I had to abandon all thoughts of driving home).

Upstairs, the house stretches out, the two wings merging through wide corridors. Jane and Edward are slowly restoring these upper rooms. Some are finished, and perfect. As elsewhere, vibrant colours and patterns combine with plainer moments: a grey bathroom is soothing; the guest bedroom-cum-dressing room elegant with a hand-painted Chinese wallpaper. Other rooms are not yet begun. It gives us hope to know that even such masters of making a supremely comfortable home don't do everything in one go.

LOULOU DE LA FALAISE

THE DINING ROOM

Page 114 Edward and Jane's dining room is painted a rich tomato red; the doors are a slubby grey. The round dining table is overlooked by one of Edward's recent purchases: an extraordinary portrait by the Dorset artist George Spencer Watson of his wife Hilda. The colour of the dress perfectly and coincidentally reflects the colour of the walls. Jane's dining table is decorated with bunches of home-grown jewel-like dahlias, and laid with an array of nineteenth-century china and glass.

A CORNER OF THE SITTING ROOM

Page 117 A quiet corner of the sitting room, akin to a Dutch still-life painting: a deep Howard chair made even more comfortable by squashy velvet cushions, a broad Delft bowl, and a spare, almost minimal, collection of paintings. In the hallway beyond, cool grey light contrasts with the faded tobacco tones of the sitting-room walls. Edward installed the black-and-white encaustic tile floor recently, but it has the timeless quality that exemplifies Manor Farmhouse.

THE SITTING ROOM

Page 118–119 The view from the hall across to the sitting-room French doors, which lead to a glass and metal lean-to, recently added by Edward to the south wall of the house to provide shelter for Jane's collection of tender plants. A grey marble Regency fire surround is perfectly proportioned for this modest, square room. Like Edward, I prefer my fire irons to be steel, not brass. On the mantelshelf is a collection of beautiful paraphernalia. Everything in the room belongs against one another; nothing jars.

SITTING-ROOM DETAILS

Pages 120 A sparkling lacquer cabinet with extraordinarily fine detailing provides a fireworks display in the corner of the sitting room; above, more explosions in the form of dried allium heads spilling out of a blue china bowl. *Page 121* This corner of the room is filled with magical pieces of English furniture that somehow, gently, make us feel at home—perhaps because they are so at home themselves. Jane fills the house with flowers from the garden.

THE SNUG

Pages 122–123 A small space, the snug is packed with furniture and books— this is Edward's architectural and historical furniture reference library, and his desk sits in the corner by a window. Jane's is on the opposite wall. The chairs are time-worn, with their original upholstery, and sit on a richly faded red wool rug. The whole impression is of a Victorian collector's study. The cushions on the sofa are by William de Morgan, available from Fine Cell Work.

THE KITCHEN

Page 124 The kitchen is in the older cottage; it has lower ceilings and casement windows. A scrubbed pine table fills the room, with a collection of comfortable mismatched chairs. The sink is an old Belfast with simple brass pillar taps.
Page 125 At one end of the kitchen is this giant cabinet, still with its original green paint, which holds all crockery, glasses and food. Enormous original slabs of blue lias stone are on the floor.

THE LANDING AND BEDROOMS

Page 126 The bedroom corridor is white, with dark grey joinery. Tom and Fleur's bedrooms reveal the children's passions—Tom is already a successful antiques dealer, putting all his profits into tribal collections; Fleur is a talented rider and multicoloured trophies hang from her four-poster bed.
Page 126 below right and page 127 Edward and Jane's bedroom is painted a moody red. The chartreuse bench provides a light touch at the foot of the bed. On a chest of drawers, blue-and-white china forms a perfectly composed still life.

THE GUEST BEDROOM AND BATHROOM

Page 128 The guest bathroom is painted a dark blue-grey that could be gloomy but is a rich, complex colour, set alive by a collection of framed engravings. The old cast-iron bathtub is deep and long enough to get lost in.
Page 129 In the guest bedroom, the walls are papered with a hand-painted blue-grey Chinese paper by de Gournay. On the wall opposite the door stands a beautiful lacquered chest with Chinese vases.

THE DRESSING ROOM AND THE HOUSE

Page 130 The guest bedroom doubles as Edward's dressing room and has cupboards painted a flat mushroom-pink colour. Above the fireplace is a bold Regency convex mirror. The rush carpet is from Felicity Irons.
Page 131 A view of Manor Farmhouse from the east; a brick Regency façade with a slate roof and wide sash windows. To the left is the iron and glass plant shelter and steps leading to Jane's borders. Beyond are the outbuildings.

The Temple

A MASTERCLASS IN CLASSIC DECORATION

Veere Grenney is the pre-eminent English decorator of his generation, one of that rare stable of designers who, over a long career, develop a beautiful and distinctive style entirely of their own. Veere trained with Mary Fox Linton, later becoming a director at Sibyl Colefax & John Fowler, and with this impeccable pedigree set up his own company some twenty years ago. His interiors are (to the cognoscenti) immediately recognizable, with their architectural lines and soft palette of pinks, greys, lemon yellow, dove blue and occasional dramatic flourishes of dark olive and earth brown. Veere has a contemporary sensibility but an astonishing and encyclopedic understanding of history and tradition. Above all, his rooms are supremely luxurious and comfortable—which one cannot always say of well-decorated houses. Everything is thought about; everything works.

I have known Veere and his partner, David Oliver, for some years now. They are kind and unbelievably generous, but with a wicked sense of humour that stops it all getting too serious (as, in these surroundings, it could). David was an interior designer who set up his own highly successful eponymous paint company (earning the title 'the Rock Star of Color' from the *New York Times* along the way). Endlessly seeking new challenges, he is now turning his talents to interior photography. He is father to two children, Edward and Cosmo, whom he cites (alongside Veere) as the greatest influences in his life. Veere is a New Zealander; David is Australian. I find this interesting, because together they have defined so closely what English design and decoration means today. Perhaps, after all, there is something more English about the former colonies than England itself.

At Veere and David's tiny but grand retreat in Suffolk, called The Temple, that sense of Englishness is distilled and strengthened to create a microcosm of classic decoration. Standing at the end of a long, dark canal, the house is a fragment of a much larger Georgian estate. Coming here is like experiencing a dream world, which is entered by stepping elegantly through the looking glass.

The Temple has pedigree. It was designed in the 1760s by the architect Sir Robert Taylor as the fishing lodge of a grand house—Sir John Soane's first country house—tragically demolished in the 1950s. Today, only the stone porch of the great mansion stands, and the parkland, with its vast trees and fragmentary memories of a once-great landscape (including an old and overgrown walled garden) has a soulful, melancholy air.

Thankfully, in the 1960s, this tiny building was rescued by David Hicks (the great interior decorator and hero to us all), becoming the first in a long succession of ravishing houses that Hicks restored. Hicks camped out at The Temple, using the building as a summer retreat, without central heating or amenities. Later, the decorator Charles Beresford-Clark took the house on and restored it, creating in the main room a magnificent pale butter interior with vast fringed curtains and classic decoration in the Colefax and Fowler tradition. Veere's tenure at The Temple began some thirty years ago, and the house now has the settled air that comes from being the subject of complete and loving care over time.

It is approached by a quiet, hidden country lane. At a dip in the road, you get a first startling glimpse of the orange-ochre walls and the deeply overhanging Tuscan eaves of the portico. But little of the house is revealed. You enter the landscape through a secret garden, and arrive at the great show façade as if entering another world. The long canal stretches away to the east, shimmering, reflecting the cool grey Suffolk sky. It is like a piece of Italy dropped into the agrarian landscape of rural East Anglia.

Inside, the building is one large classical room. A single window faces on an axis down the canal; on the opposite wall is a generous west-facing octagonal bay window, a motif that recurs in Sir Robert Taylor's other great Georgian houses. The room is airily light and tall-ceilinged, with beautiful plasterwork decoration, and a delicate fireplace and overmantel. The walls are a pink specially mixed for the room by David. The east wall has two great half-round niches that Veere, characteristically, has filled with trees in old terracotta pots—dressing down just when others might dress up. It is a magical room—not just as a piece of architecture, or even as a piece of decoration—but as a place for conversation and laughter in the evening, over gins-and-tonics and cocktails and small silver trays of nuts and olives, as the westering sun gently sets and The Temple casts a lengthening Prussian-blue shadow across the grey watery canal.

Downstairs is a tiny dining room, with the *oeil-de-boeuf* window introduced by Hicks (and designed by the classical architect Raymond Erith) to bring light to this lower floor. The window has a view across the water; in the morning, sunlight streams in. Here, Veere has installed a carefully planned kitchen, with everything needed to produce a stream of delicious breakfasts, lunches and dinners. Beyond, in one of the triangular, pedimented side wings, is the bedroom; the opposite wing contains a generous staircase to the room on the *piano nobile*, or first floor.

A tiny guest bedroom and the boys' room are located in a side cottage. The decoration here retains that blend of simplicity and luxurious sophistication that is Veere and David's hallmark: softly painted grey walls, carefully hung pictures, interesting furniture, rush flooring, Beni Ourain rugs and—always, always—a pot of freshly grown scented flowers from the glasshouse.

Veere and David have a house in London, and for years now they have been creating a new house of astounding beauty in Tangier that defies all expectations. But the Tangerine dream is for another day. For now, let us revel in their Suffolk retreat, gently absorbing the lessons from this masterclass of classic decoration.

THE TEMPLE AND CANAL

Page 134 The serene neoclassical façade of The Temple is reflected in the steely grey waters of the wide, long canal that stretches away in front of it. The house's striking ochre walls introduce a shot of Italy into the cool autumnal tones of the Suffolk landscape. Deeply overhanging Tuscan eaves are comforting and friendly. A single tall window overlooks the canal from the first-floor salon; below, in the arched recess, is an *oeil-de-boeuf* window designed by Raymond Erith for a previous owner, David Hicks.

THE DRAWING ROOM

Page 137 The canal stretches away as if to infinity, creating a view that is hard to tear yourself away from. Veere has dressed the windows in exuberant ruched blinds; rush matting lines the floor, and in the foreground is one of his Brooke armchairs upholstered in his own pink quilted silk. The masterstroke is the bright Chinese-yellow silk cushion—without it, the room would feel strangely diminished. A nineteenth-century French Empire table stands alongside the chair, with a bunch of roses from the garden.

THE SITTING ROOM

Pages 138–139 A serenely elegant room in shades of soft pink, mushroom, grey, cream, taupe: here is a fine example of an interior to which nothing can be added and nothing taken away without harming the whole. This is why, for me, Veere's rooms at the The Temple, which are full of his fabrics and designs, are the epitome of classic English decoration. An Empire chair stands by the fire. The original 1950s Arredoluce lamp was bought at auction in New York.

THE KITCHEN AND DINING ROOM

Page 140 Veere designed the kitchen, using the plainest cabinetry, white handmade tiles and a simple marble top. The woodwork is painted in a slubby brown-grey, Tarlatan, from Paint & Paper Library.
Page 141 The ground floor has low ceilings and the simplest, cottage-like interiors. A dining table has been placed in the middle of the octagonal bay, with views over the water; the table is French and the chairs are Hepplewhite.

THE BATHROOM AND BEDROOMS

Pages 142–143 Veere and David know how to create wonderfully comfortable guest rooms full of interesting objects and pictures. In each room is a clay flowerpot borrowed from the greenhouse, containing paperwhites in winter and spring, and scented geraniums in summer and autumn. The pair of black iron bedsteads was found at the Bed Bazaar in nearby Framlingham. The four-poster bed is eighteenth-century Swedish, but Veere has copied it many times for clients; a painting by Teddy Millington-Drake hangs on the adjacent wall.

COUNTRY HOUSES

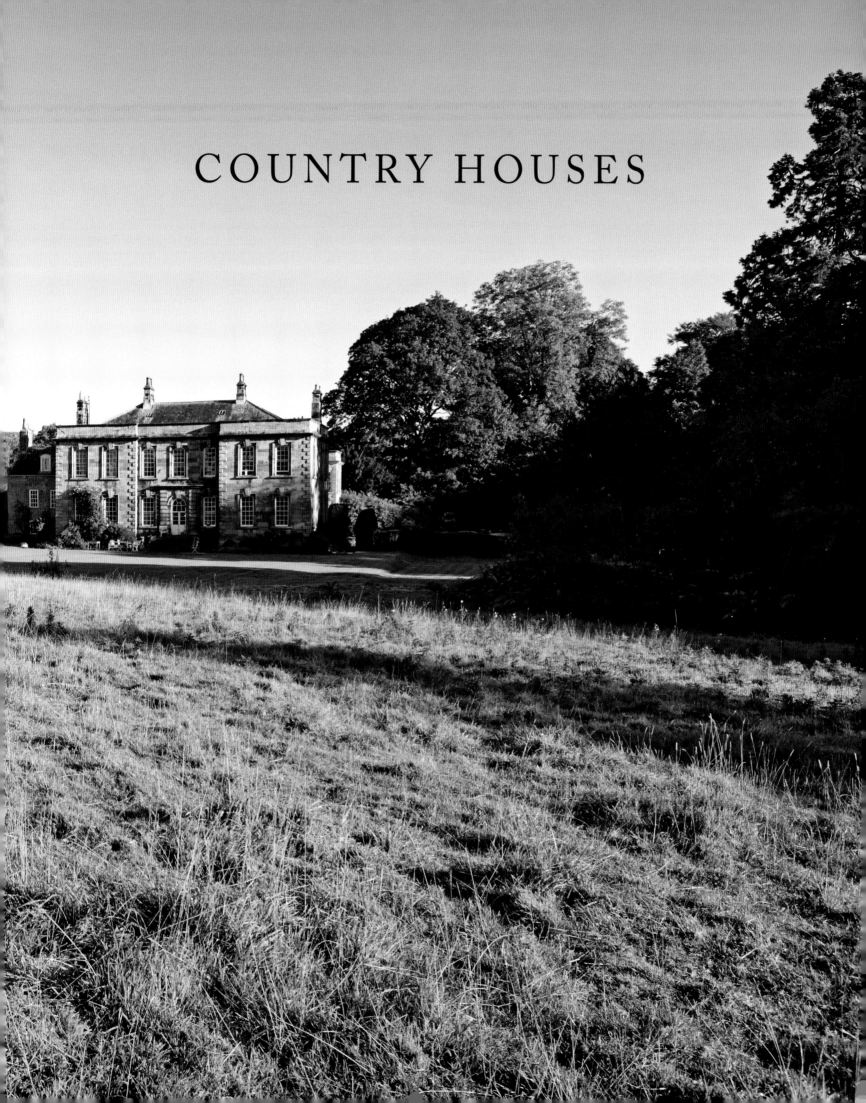

In Northumberland

THE TIMELESSNESS OF ENGLISH DECORATION

There is a romance to Northumberland that I find intoxicating. This is a rugged landscape of hill farms and market towns, of tiny, stone-built villages, and of the wide, windswept coastline where England faces the steely North Sea, guarded by the great castles of Bamburgh and Lindisfarne and bounded to the north by the Scottish border. It is a place that has known its share of turmoil and struggle. But there are softer sides too: generous people, beautiful buildings, richly thriving and unspoiled towns, and fine countryside and wooded valleys looked after by the proprietors of a few great estates where feudal loyalties and obligations still survive. London, and the din and roar of the south, feels very far away.

In a wide river valley there is a village that exemplifies this feudal history, lying on a lonely road leading from nowhere and going to nowhere else in particular. At one end of the village, behind a modest set of gates and a handsome, dilapidated farm range, stands a house of such extreme beauty that I feel confident in saying it is one of the finest small country houses in Britain. A wonderful, chaotically happy family are the occupants; it is their ancestral home, inherited on the maternal side, and it is hard to imagine a more romantic image of England than we find here.

Stone-built, with a boldly symmetrical classical façade of seven bays and a raised ground floor overlooking rolling grazed parkland, the house has evolved over several different periods of construction. It began life as a simple vernacular farmhouse, sixteenth or seventeenth century in origin, quite humble in character. In the mid-eighteenth century, in a style fashionable some thirty years earlier in London, a perfect classical wing was added to the south. It is built of grey Northumberland sandstone with richly carved quoins and window surrounds with exuberant keystones in the Baroque manner of James Gibbs, the early Georgian architect. No one knows who designed this ravishing façade.

Later, in the nineteenth century, the house was extended again, in a style that matches the Georgian original but without its grace and vigour, as all the prerequisites of Victorian country-house life—billiard room, boot room, gun room and a great array of bedrooms and bathrooms—were added. The house rambles from one wing to the next, with flights of steps leading up and down, this way and that. Its architecture has grandeur yet recalls the modest scale of a doll's house. Nothing is too large or overwhelming; it is the ideal country house.

The châtelaine is a woman of great character and beauty, who brings wit, humour, and an irrepressible effervescence to the place. She makes it all work through skill and resourcefulness—one minute renting the place to fashion photographers from *Vogue,* the next getting down on her hands and knees to weed the garden path, or dashing into town in her Kelly-green Citroën 2CV to buy a spare part for the tractor and returning, effortlessly, to rustle up (from nowhere) dinner for ten. Nothing is too much for this indomitable force of nature.

Upon inheriting the house, she promptly moved the kitchen—previously banished to a remote service wing—to the sunny and light-filled great hall, bringing it firmly into the heart of the place, the ancient AGA seeming quite at home amongst the bolection panelling and sash windows. Next door, the oak-panelled library had a fully working pub bar installed, complete with bar stools—the perfect place to sit and chat through the night. She has a brilliance that flows through every pore of the building.

The house has many rooms where the decoration has not been touched for a hundred years or more. Curtains dangle increasingly threadbare from Edwardian curtain poles. In the Victorian wing is a great cast-iron bathtub and shower, still working as well as the day it was installed. Original William Morris paper lines the billiard-room walls, mostly faded now to a pale red-grey after exposure to a century of sunshine, while in the shadowy corners of the room it retains its dark-red hue. This is decoration like no other. It cannot be made up, or bought, or even designed; it has been preserved as much by economic necessity as by desire. It is rare to find a house as beautiful as this that remains so untouched.

Chaos is everywhere, not always kept at bay, and here, too, lies part of the charm of these unhurried rooms. It becomes more extreme the further into the house you burrow; there are rooms groaning with thousands of pieces of china, stored by generations, nothing thrown away; attic rooms piled with old trunks, or hanging with racks of Victorian clothes, as if we have stepped into a magical dressing-up box. There is something of Narnia to these rooms, as though you can pull apart the fur coats and hunting pinks and step through into some other land, where time moves in a different space and landscape.

The garden is likewise held in a resting, watchful state, balanced between structure and disarray. Steps are thick with moss; ancient Victorian stone balustrades crumble gently; dipping ponds at the intersection of old stone paths have deep, dark and limpid water where newts and frogs thrive beneath the lily leaves. Everywhere nature abounds and is cherished. At dusk, wandering through the garden, looking back at the gentle vernacular wing with the classical house beyond, it is if we are in another time, at a house forgotten by the twenty-first century. And the old ancestral home smiles and breathes a contented sigh, before settling for just another starry night in the hundred and fifty thousand since it was built.

THE LIBRARY

Page 148 In a corner of the library, an armchair with a faded-pink slipcover catches the afternoon light by the warmth of a roaring fire. The coral-and-grey floral cushion is a chintz from the 1950s; a Chinese-yellow glazed lamp provides a flash of colour. The curtains, like many in the house, have survived from the Edwardian era, but the owner has wisely decided that they must never be changed. The stone fireplace is lined with Delft tiles and has a curious dragon-like beast carved into its lintel.

THE DRAWING-ROOM FIREPLACE

Page 151 Another fireplace, another detail: this time, it is the sensational panelling that adorns the drawing room (shown also on later pages). Original to the house, the panelling is early eighteenth century in style despite the later date when it was made. It is richly modelled, with great Ionic fluted pilasters and bold bolection panels. Country-house clutter—Edwardian photographic portraits, Staffordshireware and other random bits and pieces—lines the mantelshelf of the Georgian stone fireplace.

THE DRAWING ROOM

Pages 152-153 In this serene room, with squashy sofas and armchairs ranged around the wide fireplace, a corgi lies in his basket and a huge Turkey rug covers the floor. The curtains are in a printed linen with a bold, multicoloured design. Slight smoke stains on the walls are the consequence of a chimney fire that occurred when a famous photographer was doing a fashion shoot in the room; lighting the fire caused the chimney to go up and the room to fill with smoke. The owner liked the look so much that she decided not to repaint.

THE STAIRCASES

Pages 154–155 This is a house of stairs, leading up and down to different levels and from one wing to the next. The stairwells are painted a rich sunny yellow, which counters the cold Northumbrian light and brings warmth to the heart of the home. The main staircase is elegant, late eighteenth century, with a detailed Palladian window overlooking the courtyard to the rear. Secondary stairs feature a mixture of panelling and old oak balusters. A glimpse into the oak-panelled dining room reveals that it is lined entirely with portraits of dogs.

THE KITCHEN AND PANTRY

Pages 156–157 When she inherited the house, the owner took the bold and sensible decision to move the kitchen from a chilly wing to the old entrance hall, facing south-west across the park. Sunshine streams in from morning to late afternoon. At one end is a cream-coloured AGA; at the other is an old Georgian fireplace with comfortable armchairs—perfect for an afternoon nap. The pantry, next door, is idyllic; it has not been touched for decades, and is a sublime example of timeless country-house decoration.

THE BILLIARD ROOM

Pages 158–159 In the Victorian wing, the walls of the billiard room are covered in a distinctive block-printed paper featuring flowers and foliage—a Morris & Co. original—whose colours have faded in the sun. Lovely piles of junk fill the corners of this room; elegant shades hang on long, silk-lined cords over the full-sized billiard table with its green baize cover.

THE BEDROOMS

Pages 160–161 The bedrooms are decorated in sublime Edwardian country-house style with generous beds, pretty furniture, floral wallpapers and delicate carpets. Untouched for a century, the rooms are now faded almost beyond belief; they recall a look known as 'shabby chic', which gained favour about twenty years ago. When it is faked up from nowhere, this is a style that makes my skin creep. Here it is real—and perfect.

THE EXTERIOR

Pages 162–163 In front of the austere classical façade sits the owner's trusty leaf-green 2CV, creating an effect that is as unexpected and unpretentious as her interiors. Through a graceful and alluring wrought-iron garden gate, tucked between stone pillars and a pair of enormous yew hedges, along which fantastical topiary is formed, is a startling view over the Northumberland country—garden, then parkland, giving way to long views of the hills beyond.

Herringston

AN ANCESTRAL HOME IN HARDY COUNTRY

Just to the south of Dorchester, the Roman county town of Dorset, is a dreamy, hidden, watery valley that feels lost in time, barely touched by the modern world. On the quiet road that snakes through this meandering chalk valley, at a sharp bend, is a pair of low stone gate piers marking a long, straight drive that leads to a manor house of rare age and venerable history. This is Herringston, home of the Williams family since the early sixteenth century, and lived in today by Raymond and Pollyann Williams. Herringston is the perfect sort of country house; just like its owners, it is gentle, quiet and unassuming. It has an air—like the valley surrounding it, with its great lime and yew trees, and grazing fields with clumps of ancient oak—of eternal and unhurried timelessness.

The Williams love and understand this place deeply, and believe that little should be touched or disturbed in the name of progress. They cherish the lichen-encrusted façade, with its grey-purple blotchiness and time-worn patina (that can never be made up), while at the same time ensuring that everything is perfectly maintained in a well-measured cycle of repair. So the windows are freshly painted, but nothing else is touched. It is rare, these days, to find owners so sensitive to the needs and voices of a building. Perhaps it is the house's great longevity that has brought them to this understanding.

Herringston is a house of many parts. At its core are fragments of a fourteenth-century building, although nothing visible now remains earlier than the sixteenth century. Three hundred years of building extensions, including early Georgian, Regency and Victorian additions, have left their mark, yet everything is harmonious. From the outside the house is a little austere, although I love its silvery-grey plainness. But it is inside that the house reveals treats of astonishing richness and beauty.

You ascend a wide, generous staircase to reach, on the first floor, the Great Chamber, one of the most ravishing rooms I have ever been in. Here, time stands still. We are in a place that resonates with the ancient heartbeat of the old kingdom of Wessex. The wide, barrel-vaulted ceiling is decorated with astounding moulded Jacobean plasterwork, dating to the early seventeenth century, and thought to be the work of itinerant Italian plasterers.

A series of panels on the ceiling itself contains designs of remarkable legendary and heraldic beasts, of an angel, the Royal Arms, the Prince of Wales's feathers and initials C. P., shells and a pelican, all surrounded by a framework of panels with scrolls of foliage, fruit and flowers of an intense richness—and with all the beauty of an illustrated florilegium, so specific are the plants depicted.

Three pendentive bosses hang down to support chandeliers; the central one is populated with young boys climbing up to steal apples from a tree, their feet hanging down from the brackets. There are examples of love and humour in this ceiling as well as symbolism. The whole is reminiscent of the Arts and Crafts work at Wardington (see pages 180–199); design, craft, meaning and making deftly span the centuries.

Herringston is more than one exceptional room, though. I love its Georgian and Regency additions, with boldly bolection-panelled interiors, an elegant mid-Georgian dining room, painted a soft ochre and hung with family portraits, and the early nineteenth-century rooms added to the entrance front in a restrained neoclassical style.

There are few more beautiful rooms than Raymond's book-lined study. Raymond and Pollyann have gently refreshed these rooms yet they have an untouched feel about them, with faded Edwardian wallpapers and the original drab olive-green paintwork on the walls. The bedrooms are calm spaces—perfect country-house rooms with that peculiar mix of un-done-up chintzy clutter that defies any decorative style. In the late nineteenth century, a service wing was added to the east, and its corridors and storage rooms are walled from floor to ceiling in delicious buttercup-yellow glazed tiles—an astonishingly decorative choice, making one feel that throughout its long history this must have been a contented, happy house.

The servants' wing overlooks a walled kitchen garden of great age, although not still in full production, and here Pollyann has laid out flower beds, herb beds and lawns in between *allées* of gnarled and twisted old apple trees. The gardens are simple but serene. On the west front is the old Victorian glasshouse, the ultimate dreamlike conservatory; a mossy, damp space filled to the brim with pelargoniums, scented geraniums, lilies and jasmine, and an ancient lead cistern that houses a thriving colony of frogs.

February is a time of great beauty at Herringston, when the grounds are carpeted with thousands of snowdrops. At snowdrop time, the gate on the drive is left open for visitors, and an honesty box invites donations to the local hospice. Raymond has a letter in his family archive dating from the early eighteenth century that was written by a recently arrived bride of Herringston to her sister, in which she describes how the people of Dorchester come out to the house each spring and walk down the drive to admire the snowdrops.

Raymond and Pollyann's daughter Sophia and her husband are good friends of Charlie and mine, and her brother Adair now assists Raymond in running the estate—alongside his fascinating but rather more secretive work as a leading inventor for Dyson. There is a self-effacing modesty to this whole family, quietly settled in this place for so long, simultaneously belonging to a harmonious, unbroken tradition while facing the future with energy, verve and confidence.

THE STUDY

Page 166 Raymond Williams's study has a timeless feel. It is lined with old leatherbound books on simple painted shelves that have begun to sag slightly from heavy use. The paper is faded and Edwardian, but the room is Regency, with a fine narrow plaster cornice. The carpet is a nineteenth-century leaf pattern. But the *pièce de résistance* is the nineteenth-century cock-fighting chair in scarlet leather, perfectly illuminated in the grey north light.

THE ENTRANCE HALL

Page 169 The hall at Herringston dates to the Regency period, with a delicate cornice and three elegant centred arches leading to the hall beyond. Marble busts of Williams ancestors frame the approach, while country-house ephemera and old mahogany hall chairs line the walls. The room is painted a drab olive green in a chalky paint that may be original. The stone-flagged floor, polished to a perfect finish over the years, is warmed by Turkish runners.

THE GREAT CHAMBER

Pages 170–171 This ravishing first-floor room is the principal interior at Herringston. Created in the seventeenth century by itinerant Italian craftsmen, the ceiling is cast into relief and shadow by light from the great south-facing gothic window. Pendentives hang down to support chandeliers. A faded collection of Edwardian armchairs upholstered in chintz is ranged around the room; dark furniture, smoky oak-panelled walls, and interesting collections create a penumbral, chiaroscuro effect.

THE HALL, DINING ROOM AND LARDER

Page 172 The double-height, yellow-painted hall is lined with portraits and tapestries; on the north wall is an arched opening to the stair landing above. The dining room is a mellow space, with a set of fine mahogany furniture and walls hung with Williams' family portraits in gilt frames.

Page 173 The east wing was built in the late nineteenth century and the walls of all the back offices were lined with canary-yellow glazed tiles. Deep slate shelves make a repository for a huge collection of china and glass.

THE BEDROOMS AND BATHROOM

Pages 174–175 Here are examples of true country-house decoration: joyous, time-worn, uncomplicated—a look that would be impossible to achieve today. The wallpaper is late nineteenth century. The cream-painted bathroom with its cast-iron bathtub, linoleum floor and green-and-white-striped curtains has the perfect blend of austerity and Edwardian comfort that characterized the English country-house look until very recently, when some people foolishly started trying to imitate the experience of a hotel at home.

THE CONSERVATORY

Pages 176–177 The conservatory, added to the west wing in the late nineteenth century, is one of the most beautiful rooms at Herringston. Overflowing with jasmine, pelargoniums and mock-orange, the room has a heavenly scent. Stone flags have become mossy and green with age. A cistern in the corner contains a flourishing colony of frogs. An ancient table has lived here for a long time, and four rattan chairs are faded to perfection by the sunlight.

Wardington

Wardington Manor lies in the dip of a lane in a small village on the far fringe of North
Oxfordshire, in that ever-so-slightly remote part of the country where the creamy grey
limestone of the Cotswolds gives over to the rich orange sandstone of Northamptonshire.
The house is announced to the village by a vast pair of classical gate piers that hint at the
delights beyond. Through ancient wrought-iron gates is a glimpse of a wide, perfectly flat
lawn and the ancient, rambling stone manor house beyond.

But opposite is another pair of gates, leading to a field filled with a remarkable,
almost year-round crop of English flowers, which are, perhaps, our first engagement
with Wardington. The owner, Bridget Elworthy, is an extraordinary and vivacious New
Zealander; she and her husband Forbes are close friends of my husband Charlie, and as
such have become great new friends of my own. In 2014 Bridget, with Henrietta Courtauld,
established The Land Gardeners, and the pair design gardens, research soil and plant
health, teach courses, and supply—from this small corner of Oxfordshire—seasonally
grown cut flowers to a small number of specialist London florists. The flower field at
Wardington is one of the most beautiful places I have visited. It has the perfect
combination of creative chaos and austere practicality.

These two characteristics perhaps best describe the whole of Wardington, where
rooms are at once restrained and simple, yet overflowing with a generosity of touch and
a richness of colour and texture. Forbes has a deep reverence for the history of the place;
Bridget an effortless ability to put together rooms in a way that is nonchalant, in which a
recent junk-shop find is placed against dark, ancient panelling and both sing as a result.

The house is sixteenth century with extensive Arts and Crafts additions, notably the remarkable chalky-white moulded plaster decorations that line the walls of the hall and main staircase. Executed in the 1920s by the artistic Irish beauty Molly Wells, they are testament to an enduring Cotswold tradition of making by hand that lasted throughout the early twentieth century. More recently, in 2004, the house suffered a disastrous fire; the skill and sensitivity with which it was repaired and restored by the then owners, Lord and Lady Wardington, is testament to the continuing vitality of these skills.

Wardington is a large, rambling house, where staircases lead up one way, through narrow rooms and wide rooms, and down another. It can be confusing to understand the geography of the place, with wings of various ages and where nothing is level, steps up and down wherever you go. Doors lead this way and that, and everywhere we catch glimpses through leaded-light windows to the expansive Edwardian gardens beyond.

Bridget has painted the whole house plain white. The floors are oak, often covered with large areas of hand-woven rush matting; the walls in many rooms are of oak panelling, stained dark or limewaxed to a soft pale grey. Empty, these rooms would be entirely neutral, like a Danish interior painted by Hammershøi—in tones of pure white, grey or dark brown. But the house is infused with rich colour. Throughout, Bridget has brought her perfect mix of imperfect bits and pieces: old four-poster beds with ancient strips of fabric pinned to the tester; deep chairs with fading chintz slipcovers and overflowing with pink or red satin cushions; wobbly chests of drawers; boldly painted furniture; and everywhere, of course, bunches of flowers picked from the gardens.

Bridget's gardens are dreamlike, Edwardian in character, as if we have just stepped back into that quiet hot summer before the unhurried world of the country house was shattered by the declaration of war in August 1914. Contained by tall stone walls and dark yew hedges, the flowerbeds are planted with an ebullient mix of English perennials that grow rampantly across lawns and paths. The garden feels permanently on the brink of chaos, overflowing with productivity. At dawn most mornings, an army of pickers makes its way through the gardens and flower field to collect the freshest blooms. A long walk leads through a leafy shrubbery to a secret lake, where a wooden boathouse watches silently over the still waters.

Above all, Wardington is a family home, filled with children, laughter and noise. The house is open to all comers, made welcome by the Elworthys' own inimitable generosity. The kitchen table at breakfast on a Sunday morning is lined with an assembly of guests from around the world, each blinking with unexpected pleasure at their arrival at this little corner of paradise, and at a table laden with blueberries and bread, jars of cereals and nuts, freshly laid eggs, and with candles burning in the sunlight streaming through a wide garden door.

A CORNER OF THE HALL

Page 180 In the entrance hall at Wardington, Bridget Elworthy pairs a bucket of foxgloves, picked from the walled garden, with an old classical bust. Calm light falls from a leaded-light window onto the remarkable plasterwork that covers every wall of the ground-floor halls and corridors. Molly Wells was the plasterer, an Arts and Crafts beauty, whose romantic connections to the owner of Wardington in the 1920s was recently uncovered by Mary Miers for *Country Life* magazine. She cast the bold chevron pattern in panels.

THE STAIRCASE

Page 183 At the opposite end of the house is this beautiful staircase; an ancient oak stair and newel that leads to the south-west wing bedrooms overlooking the garden. The extraordinary profile of the newel is silhouetted against yet more extraordinary plasterwork by Wells. An oak-panelled door with seventeeth-century detailing, half ajar, provides a tantalizing view to the winter sitting room. Wardington is a house of glimpsed vistas.

A VIEW OF THE HALL

Pages 184–185 This wide view of the hall shows the effect of the plasterwork at Wardington, which covers every surface of these rooms. It is an astonishing tour de force made even more beautiful by the softest, filtered light falling through windows shrouded by climbing plants in the courtyard. Old stone flags with slate diamonds line the floor. In a space like this, Bridget understands exactly how low key the furnishings need to be. The door on the left leads to the dining room.

THE DINING ROOM

Pages 186–187 The dining room is a serene space, with dark, oak-panelled walls designed by the twentieth-century architect Clough Williams-Ellis. You can see the lushly planted garden through the cross-mullioned, leaded-light windows. Bridget throws a huge, plain white antique linen sheet, bought in France, over the dining table, and simple coconut matting covers the floor. The whole house is filled with flowers freshly picked from the garden.

THE LIBRARY

Page 188 Details of the library. Steps lead down to the winter sitting room that we glimpsed from the staircase, above. In a sitting room next door, Bridget has hung a richly coloured crewel-work tapestry across an entire wall. A battered old Edwardian armchair sits by the grand piano.
Page 189 The library is a marvellous Arts and Crafts room created in the 1920s for 'Montie' Pease, later Lord Wardington. The oak-framed ceiling came from a building in Theydon Bois, Essex. The panelling is lime waxed.

THE WINTER SITTING ROOM

Pages 190 191 The winter sitting room or snug is dark and cosy, with deep Edwardian sofas grouped around a wide stone fireplace that may have been designed by Clough Williams-Ellis. A bright scarlet slipper chair is from Soane Britain, together with a cushion in their Damascus Stripe. The generous ottoman is piled with books and magazines; this is alluring and comfortable country-house decoration of a room you want to spend time in. Blowsy peonies from the cutting garden fill jars abundantly.

THE KITCHEN AND FLOWER ROOM

Pages 192–193 The kitchen is a warm-hearted room, with a wide table around which all family life takes place. Bridget's kitchen style can be distilled into a successful recipe: a cream AGA, white curtains in front of the cupboards and Carrara marble counters with white tiles and a simple shelf above. Throw in a huge, vividly painted dresser, and season with a generous pinch of clutter. Nearby is the flower room, the heart of her business, filled with Victorian jugs, Fulham ware pottery, and buckets of flowers picked from the cutting field.

THE BEDROOMS

Pages 194–195 Staying at Wardington is a wonderful experience, sleeping in ancient four-posters or beds with elaborate half-testers. Every bedroom has old bits of furniture, mainly junk-shop or country auction-house finds, laden with interesting books and overwhelming bunches of flowers. A white-panelled guest bathroom has an enormous antique cast-iron tub and curtains in Pineapple Frond by Soane. It's the perfect room for a lingering bath, by candlelight, at dusk on a summer's evening with the windows wide open.

THE HOUSE AND GARDEN

Page 196 Wardington has famous gardens that Bridget has extended and added to with her customary energy. At the far reach of the garden, a shady walk of shrub planting leads to a hidden lake, complete with boathouse. Outside the library she pulls out old Edwardian armchairs in the summer.
Page 197 A view from the vegetable garden back towards the many-gabled house with its orangey-red North Oxfordshire stone and tall chimneys. Oriel windows provide views from the bedrooms across the garden.

Trematon Castle

FLAMBOYANT HAPPINESS IN CORNWALL

Where Cornwall meets Devon, at a remarkable and strategic site overlooking the River Tamar, is a house of dazzling beauty that, from the moment you arrive, takes your breath away. It is the home of garden designers Julian and Isabel Bannerman and, just like the Bannermen themselves, it fizzes with energy and fireworks, providing a perfect conclusion to our tour of English houses.

Julian and Isabel started working together in 1983 and over a thirty-year career they have created some of the finest gardens in Britain, working at a number of aristocratic estates and, most famously, assisting the Prince of Wales with his remarkable gardens at Highgrove. Their designs are rich in symbol and adornment, characteristically made out of huge hewn green-oak elements, rough cut, then carved with wonderful vermiculation, of which the most dramatic example is perhaps their recent work at Arundel Castle for the Duke and Duchess of Norfolk. They draw equally from elements of Baroque garden planning and from the architectural-theatrical designs of England's first great classical architect Inigo Jones, but nothing they touch feels like a museum piece. Julian and Isabel create a living, breathing, romantic classicism that is resolutely of its time. Their classical framework provides the setting for lavish, richly toned planting, exuberant and bold, with the massed effect of thousands of tulip bulbs or great yew trees, box hedges and blowsy herbaceous borders spilling this way and that in a remarkable symphonic composition.

Trematon Castle, which has been the couple's home for the past five years, provides a suitably theatrical backdrop for their dramatic plantings, with its Regency castellated façade and a ruined medieval castle in the garden. The views to the river are unbelievable; stepping into infinity early on a misty spring morning, we imagine we are looking at the drop cloths of a great theatrical stage set.

The house is long and plain, in a commanding position facing south-east over the river. It has tall, wide sash windows through which the morning sunlight streams in. At one end is the high-ceilinged drawing room; at the other is the kitchen. In between is an enfilade of comfortable rooms flanking a broad staircase with a top-lit, double-height hall. Designed and built in the early nineteenth century by a naval man, a follower of the architect Sir John Soane, Trematon has a perfect, compact plan, which creates the feel of a grand country house but on a modest and manageable scale.

In these spaces the Bannermans have made their mark with characteristic verve. Rooms are painted burnt orange, sky blue, lime green, daffodil yellow and turquoise—rich, cheerful shades that have nothing to do with the subtle, oh-so-tasteful soft greys that have dominated English interiors for too long now. Oversized pieces of country-house furniture, collected over the decades since they first started rescuing unloved grand houses (The Ivy, Chippenham, being their first venture into Baroque living), fill rooms and provide structure. Deep sofas and armchairs are pulled in and stuffed to overflowing with cushions.

Piles of books are everywhere, and each wall is filled with pictures. Indeed, the whole house is closely hung with collection after collection—of fern prints, Regency glitter pictures, Piranesi etchings, architectural drawings, Sutherlands, antique architectural plasters, vintage typographic posters, old maps, portraits and drawings. A lifetime of collecting is represented on these walls, but at the same time nothing is static; objects and pictures migrate around the house. Many of the finest drawings are by the talented but relatively unknown interior decorator David Vicary, who lived at Kilvert's Parsonage when the Bannermans were nearby at The Ivy; he became a good friend, and Julian names him as a powerful influence. Vicary's architectural and topographical drawings, in pen, ink, gouache and watercolour, are exquisite.

The mantelshelves of the Regency marble fireplaces, original to the house, are crammed with displays by Isabel. China, candlesticks, Victorian oil lamps, vases of flowers, cards, invitations, and plastic mannequins of the Royal Family jostle for position. Everywhere there is a riot of colour, pattern, image, and interest. And then huge bunches of flowers or sweetly scented bowls of hyacinths are brought indoors from the garden or the greenhouse. The outside extends into the interior and vice versa.

Everything in this house tells a story. There is history and meaning to each object, relayed by Julian with breathless enthusiasm; provenance and romance rolled into one. It is as if the country-house aesthetic has been distilled and given a headier, more powerful scent in the combination of these two wonderful yet slightly mysterious people.

Isabel is shyer; Julian more exuberant. One feels that he is the one who comes up with the bold ideas, and she is the one who makes them happen. But Isabel has extraordinary talent in her own right, as shown in her series of serene, haunting, large-scale plant and flower portraits, taken on a scanner, in which the folds of tulip or magnolia petals or of a tightly unfurling fern frond are recorded with an almost sexual power. It is startling to come across these pictures, with their raw energy, displayed on the landing of the genteel stair hall.

Trematon is an ancient place, owned by the Duchy of Cornwall—the present Duke, Prince Charles, is of course the Bannermans' most famous client and collaborator. Into this historic location the couple have brought a refreshing energy. It is extraordinary how, after such a short tenure, they have managed to create the impression that they have lived here for ever. This is something to do with the special alchemy that the Bannermans bring to every house and garden they have touched and loved—an alchemy that results in a living, breathing classicism, which feels eternally, uniquely and timelessly English.

THE HALLWAY

Page 200 The hallway is a fine space, top-lit, with a galleried landing to a roof lantern above. Julian and Isabel have composed a suitably dramatic composition here: the table is a modern copy of an eighteenth-century painted console by Thomas Farnolls Pritchard (best remembered now as the designer of the world's first iron bridge); the original was owned by David Vicary. The stone foot was made specially for the Bannermans and is too heavy to move.

A CORNER OF THE DINING ROOM

Page 203 The dining room was painted a rich orange-red by Edward Bulmer, who decorated the house for a previous occupant. Many of the colours were chosen by him from his own range of paints and were kept by the Bannermans. Architectural drawings hang in this room, including, either side of the fireplace, handsome drawings by the Scottish Arts and Crafts architect Thomas Ross—Julian's father's uncle. A flotilla of tiny warships sails along the mantelshelf.

THE GREEN ROOM

Pages 204–205 Decorative fireworks explode in this wonderful room, which is part of a long enfilade linking the dining room with the drawing room beyond. Old upholstered chairs and sofas make it a comfortable spot to watch the TV. The fireplace is original, with cast-brass decoration; the mantelshelf is crammed with china and objects. The giant weathered-copper orb is by Christopher Wren, removed from Tom Tower in Oxford during a restoration in the 1960s.

THE DRAWING ROOM

Pages 206–207 The drawing room has a taller ceiling than the other rooms and huge sash windows that face south and east; sunlight streams in. Two huge sofas, upholstered in a shell fabric by Linda Bruce and overflowing with coral cushions, fill the space. The Bannermans have hung the walls with a rich display of engravings and paintings, many by David Vicary. The extraordinary theatrical curtains in striped yellow silk were designed by Edward Bulmer.

THE KITCHEN AND UTILITY ROOMS

Pages 208–209 The buttercup-yellow kitchen has a wide, scrubbed-pine table at one end and a large AGA, sinks and cabinets at the other, with old larders beyond. Behind the table is a glazed cabinet containing an enviable collection of Victorian ceramic jugs. In the utility room, a very tall feather duster tickles the ceiling. A startling turquoise-blue washbasin creates a bold moment in the downstairs loo, painted bright green and lined with maps and pictures.

THE MASTER BEDROOM

Pages 210–211 Julian and Isabel made up their magnificent four-poster bed years ago, cobbled together from a large Victorian wooden pelmet, and hung with bits of nineteenth-century chintz rescued from David Vicary's house. Above the fireplace, Julian has hung a collection of botanical fern engravings, framed in bright yellow; these are reflected in the ferny-green chintz armchairs below. The floor-to-ceiling sash windows offer views over the River Tamar.

THE BEDROOMS AND BATHROOMS

Pages 212–213 The Bannermans brought the bathtub from Hanham Court, their previous home near Bristol; the bathroom has a cork floor, which is about to become the most fashionable material on earth. Guest rooms are comfortable and filled with pictures and furniture, though Julian ruefully admits that people staying in the green room are liable to look a little ill. The wallpaper in the twin bedroom is reminiscent of designs by Charles Voysey.

THE CONSERVATORY AND GARDENS

Pages 214–215 The conservatory, which leads off the kitchen, is a sunny room full of flowering plants and garden clutter. In the shortest period of time, Julian and Isabel have created a richly planted, theatrical garden surrounding the old castle; medieval rampart walls lead to the ancient keep, which is now used as a shelter for domestic chickens. Exploring these gardens is like entering a child's world of adventure; they are open to the public from May to September.

Afterword

I BEGAN BY SAYING THAT THIS BOOK WAS ALL ABOUT FRIENDS.
In a strange way, as I sit here writing on the softest, quietest evening in Dorset, surrounded by piles of books, I realize that books themselves can become our friends. We refer to them time and again, for inspiration and entertainment, for affirmation or to provoke new ideas. I hope that, in some small way, this book may become a friend to some of its readers too; something to return to, one of those books that, for whatever mysterious reason, doesn't get stuck at the bottom of the pile for ever.

At home, and in my office, I am surrounded by books—so many that I'll never get around to reading the half of them. But that is not the point. They are there because they contain things that I know one day I'll find useful. And my favourite thing about picture books is that they are not really meant to be read at all. It is pertinent that Andy Warhol's famous quotation also hangs on our office wall: "I never read, I just look at pictures." I have loved writing about these houses, and their owners, and bringing life to the pages, but I am under no illusion at all that words pale in comparison to the places themselves.

I suspect that many readers will be using this book for inspiration in their own homes and I hope that some of the special rooms that we have looked at in these pages are worthy of the task. Sometimes, it is true, we look at decoration books wistfully, or even fearfully, thinking to ourselves 'my home can never be like this', and give up in despair. But I hope that is not the case here. It is true that some of the rooms we have looked at are remarkable, and are quite specific to place or person; several are the result of a lifetime's work. It is worth remembering that if you are just getting started! But equally, I believe that each contains a kernel of an idea that is in some way universal, from which you can draw happily and cheerfully—and, with increasing confidence, make your own.

Ben Pentreath, Dorset, May 2016.

Index

Design Directory

FABRICS & WALLPAPERS

Adelphi Paper Hangings
www.adelphipaperhangings.com
Beautifully printed papers.

Claremont
35 Elystan Street
London SW3 3NT
+44 (0)20 7581 9575
www.claremontfurnishing.com
The best supplier of fabric that I know.

De Gournay
112 Old Church Street
London SW3 6EP
+44 (0)20 7352 9988
www.degournay.com
Exquisite hand-painted papers.

The Dyeworks
+44 (0)1453 885036
www.dyeworks.co.uk
*Naturally dyed antique linen sheets
in a huge range of colours.*

Robert Kime
42–43 Museum Street
London WC1A 1LY
+44 (0)20 7831 6066
www.robertkime.com
*The best fabrics, wallpapers and
textiles alongside lamps and furniture.*

Ian Mankin
269/273 Wandsworth Bridge Road
London SW6 2TX
+44 (0)20 7722 0997
www.ianmankin.co.uk
Perfect tickings.

Morris & Co.
www.william-morris.co.uk
Classic English prints and papers.

Prelle
www.prelle.fr/en
Linens and plain weaves.

Svenskt Tenn
www.svenskttenn.se
Wonderful Swedish textiles.

Turnell & Gigon
Design Centre Chelsea Harbour
London SW10 0XE
+44 (0)20 7259 7280
www.turnellandgigon.com
Fine chintzes and linens.

FURNITURE

James Graham-Stewart
89–91 Scrubs Lane
London NW10 6QU
+44 (0)203 674 0404
www.jamesgraham-stewart.com
Robust nineteenth-century furniture.

Howard Chairs Ltd
30–31 Lyme Street
London NW1 0EE
+44 (0)20 7482 2156
www.howardchairs.freeserve.co.uk
The best English chairs and sofas.

Howe
93 Pimlico Road
London SW1W 8PH
+44 (0)20 7730 7987
www.howelondon.com
Perfect combinations of new and old.

Edward Hurst
The Battery
Rockbourne Road
Coombe Bissett
Salisbury
Wiltshire SP5 4LP
+44 (0)1722 718859
www.edwardhurst.com
*Edward Hurst is one of the finest
dealers of his generation.*

Max Rollitt
Yavington Barn
Lovington Lane
Avington
Hampshire SO21 1DA
+44 (0)1962 791124
www.maxrollitt.com
*Beautful antiques and perfect
reproductions.*

Soane Britain
50–52 Pimlico Road
London, SW1W 8LP
+44 (0)20 7730 6400
www.soane.co.uk
*Reproduction lighting, handsome
furniture and interesting textiles.*

Themes & Variations
231 Westbourne Grove
London W11 2SE
+44 (0)20 7727 5531
www.themesandvariations.com
Furniture by Fornasetti.

LIGHTING

Hector Finch
90 Wandsworth Bridge Road
London SW6 2TF
+44 (0)20 7731 8886
www.hectorfinch.com
Reliable, interesting lights.

Jamb
95–97 Pimlico Road
London SW1W 8PH
+ 44 (0)20 7730 2122
www.jamblimited.com
*Beautiful and perfectly made
reproduction lights and fire surrounds.*

Marianna Kennedy
3 Fournier Street
London E1 6QE
+44 (0)20 7375 2757
www.mariannakennedy.com
*Marianna's resin lights are brilliant
at enlivening an otherwise quiet space.*

Melodi Horne
www.melodihorne.com
*Lampshades in vibrant silk ikat
fabrics. We use them in many projects.*

W. Sitch
48 Berwick Street
London W1F 8JD
+ 44 (0)20 7437 3776
www.wsitch.co.uk
A treasure trove of antique lighting.

RUGS & FLOORING

The Alternative Flooring Company
www.alternativeflooring.com
*My favourite source for natural
floorcoverings.*

The Rug Company
www.therugcompany.com
*Newly designed rugs and antique
kelims that are surprisingly affordable.*

Rug Store
312 Upper Richmond Road West
London SW14 7JN
www.rugstoreonline.co.uk
Very fine and well-priced kelims.

Waveney Rush
www.waveneyrush.co.uk
English rush matting.

BATHROOMS

Balineum
www.balineum.co.uk
My first stop for bathroom accessories.

Drummonds
642 King's Road,
London SW6 2DU
+44 (0)207 376 4499
www.drummonds-uk.com
Very beautiful bathroom fittings.

PAINT

Paint & Paper Library
3 Elystan Street
London SW3 3NT
+44 (0)20 7823 7755
www.paintandpaperlibrary.com
An inspired selection of colours.

Papers and Paints
4 Park Walk
London SW10 0AD
+ 44 (0)20 7352 8626
www.papers-paints.co.uk
Beautifully made paint.

PICTURES

Abbott and Holder
30 Museum Street
London WC1A 1LH
+ 44 (0)20 7637 3981
www.abbottandholder–thelist.co.uk
The best-value dealer in London.

Jenna Burlingham
2a George Street
Kingsclere
Hampshire RG20 5NQ
+ 44 (0)1635 298855
www.jennaburlingham.com
*A fine and ever-changing stock of my
favourite sort of artists.*

FOR ABSOLUTELY EVERYTHING

Pentreath & Hall
17 Rugby Street
London WC1N 3QT
+ 44 (0)20 7430 2526
www.pentreath-hall.com
My own shop in London's Bloomsbury.

Senior commissioning editor Annabel Morgan

Location research Jess Walton

Production manager Gordana Simakovic

Art director Leslie Harrington

Editorial director Julia Charles

Publisher Cindy Richards

First published in 2016 by
Ryland Peters & Small
20–21 Jockey's Fields,
London WC1R 4BW
and
341 East 116th Street
New York, NY 10029

www.rylandpeters.com

Text copyright © Ben Pentreath 2016
Design and photographs copyright
© Ryland Peters & Small 2016

10 9 8 7 6 5 4

ISBN 978-1-84975-753-9

Picture Credits

Endpapers Herringston House in Dorset, the home of Raymond and Pollyann Williams; **2–3** Bridget Elworthy, www.thelandgardeners.com; **4** The Dorset home of Edward and Jane Hurst; **6** The London flat of Ben Pentreath and Charlie McCormick; **9** Isabel and Julian Bannerman; **10** The Dorset home of Edward and Jane Hurst; **14–31** The London flat of Ben Pentreath and Charlie McCormick; **32–45** Maisie Rowe's home in London; **46–61** The London home of Lulu Lytle of Soane Britain, www.soane.com; **62–75** Kim Wilkie's London flat; **78–95** The Dorset home and garden of Ben Pentreath and Charlie McCormick; **96–113** The home and garden of a Dorset artist; **114–133** The Dorset home of Edward and Jane Hurst; **134–145** The Temple, home of Veere Grenney; **148–167** Bridget Elworthy, www.thelandgardeners. com; **168–181** Herringston House in Dorset, the home of Raymond and Pollyann Williams; **200–217** Isabel and Julian Bannerman; **218** The Dorset home and garden of Ben Pentreath and Charles McCormick; **223** The Dorset home of Edward and Jane Hurst; **224** The home and garden of a Dorset artist.

Business Credits

I & J Bannerman Ltd
Garden designers & builders
www.bannermandesign.com
Pages 9, 200–217.

Veere Grenney Associates
1B Hollywood Road
London SW10 9HS
+44 (0)20 7351 7170
info@veeregrenney.com
www.veeregrenney.com
Pages 134–145.

Edward Hurst
Antique Dealer & Interior
Consultant
+44 (0) 7768 255557
www.edwardhurst.com
and
Jane Hurst
+44 (0) 7818 036949
janehurstgardendesign@gmail.com
Pages 4, 10, 114–133, 223.

The Land Gardeners
www.thelandgardeners.com
Pages 2–3, 148–167.

Ben Pentreath Ltd

Architecture & Decoration
3 Lamp Office Court
Lambs Conduit Street
London WC1N 3NF
+44 (0)20 7430 2424

Pentreath & Hall
17 Rugby Street
London WC1N 3QT
+44 (0)20 7430 2526

General Enquiries
Contact Zoe Wightman
enquiries@benpentreath.com
Pages 6, 14–31, 78–95, 218.

Soane Britain
50–52 Pimlico Road
London SW1W 8LP
+44 (0)20 7730 6400
www.soane.co.uk
Pages 46–61.

Kim Wilkie
16 Bank Chambers
25 Jermyn Street
London SW1Y 6HR
+44 (0)7768 874089
and
Franklin Farm
Dean Lane
Bishop's Waltham
Hampshire SO32 1FX
+44 (0)1489 891691
www.kimwilkie.com
Pages 62–75.

Acknowledgments

I began by saying this is a book about people. Without the ten generous friends who allowed Jan Baldwin and me to invade their peace and quiet, there would have been nothing to write at all. I am eternally grateful to them.

Ryland Peters & Small, notably Cindy Richards, Leslie Harrington, Annabel Morgan and Toni Kay, have been a pleasure to work with as always; Jess Walton has done a brilliant job dealing with the logistics. Jan Baldwin is the supremely assured and talented photographer who has done so much to make my vision of these buildings become real. My mother kindly read the proofs at short notice with her usual accuracy.

Finally, to my wonderful husband Charlie, who has been his usual cheery and patient self while I've tucked myself away, mainly at evenings or on weekends, to write these pages: thank you.

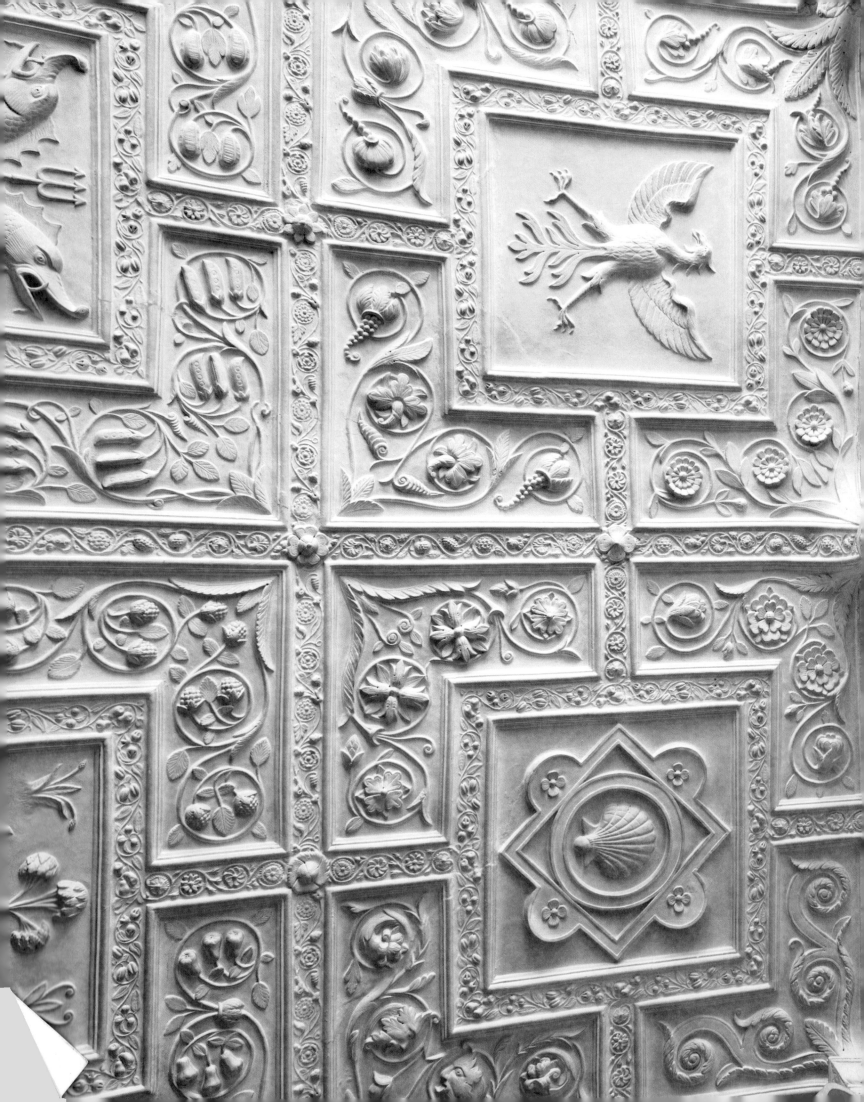